The author: Clyde Reid is Associate Director at the Institute for Advanced Pastoral Studies, Bloomfield Hills, Michigan. He was for several years Secretary of Evangelism for the Board of Homeland Ministries of the United Church of Christ.

THE EMPTY PULPIT

THE
EMPTY
PULPIT

A Study in Preaching as Communication

CLYDE REID

HARPER & ROW, PUBLISHERS

NEW YORK, EVANSTON, AND LONDON

44312

Dedicated to my friends and colleagues
in the United Church of Christ,
who welcomed me as a stranger,
accepted me,
and gave me a
home

CONTENTS

	Preface	9
	Prologue	
	THE COMPLACENT SOWER: A PARABLE	13
I.	THE PREACHING CRISIS	21
II.	PREACHING DEFENDED	34
III.	THE NEW SITUATION	46
IV.	UNDERSTANDING COMMUNICATION	63
V.	PREACHING AS COMMUNICATION	82
VI.	BEYOND PREACHING	103

PREFACE

How do we explain the curious fact of the *empty pulpit* in our time? I am not here speaking of the *empty pulpit* problem of the many churches which cannot find ministers. I speak here of the deeper and more puzzling dilemma that even when a minister occupies the pulpit it is often strangely empty—barren, sterile—to the man who sits in the pew.

The pulpit today is empty in the sense that there is often no message heard, no results seen, and no power felt. The emptiness of which I speak is an absence of meaning, a lack of relevance, a failure in communication. To be sure, this is a relative emptiness, not absolute. But it is emptiness, nevertheless.

The pulpit is an empty pulpit today from two perspectives—from the perspective of the layman and from that of the clergy. A friend, an active lay member of her church, expressed it well. When she asked what title I planned for this book, I told her, "The Empty Pulpit," and she understood immediately. Her reply: "It might as well be empty." I asked what she meant, though I thought I knew. "The pulpit might as well be empty if our ministers can't communicate with us any better than they are now," she said. A housewife said it this way: "People are not available to hear the sermon because they have switched off even before the minister begins."

It is important to note that the pulpit is equally empty from the point of view of the clergy. A friend who has preached widely in American churches recently put it like this: "I must confess that I find it more and more difficult to get into the pulpit—even when I'm up there I have a sinking feeling that it is getting *pretty empty*. I'm inclined to think the whole situation represents an artificial, indeed, an impossible and obsolete form of public address." My friend is not alone in this feeling. I have heard many ministers express similar ideas.

So we have the empty pulpit. How are we to understand this? Do we need better trained ministers? Are we simply preaching the wrong message? Or does the problem lie with the listener?

I first became concerned about the relationship between preaching and communication when, as a young pastor, I observed very little happening as a direct result of my preaching. I worked hard on my sermons, and I am sure the results were no worse than those of most of my fellow preachers. And yet, when I was honest, I could see very little concrete effect from that preaching in changed lives and changed attitudes.

For some years I have been trying to understand the preaching problem by studying the nature of communication.

If preaching is a form of communication, and we know more about communication today than ever before, then communication research may be able to help us. So I reasoned, and I have not been disappointed. I now offer some of the insights gained from my study of this problem, and invite you to ponder with me a few of their meanings for the future of preaching and the future of the churches.

This book is an attempt to cut through some of the theological verbiage with which we have surrounded preaching until it has become a Protestant "sacred cow." It is my hope that this discussion will open up the much needed dialogue on this subject and help us to see it more realistically than we have in recent years.

My earliest interest in communication can be traced back to my undergraduate years at Bradley University where I was a journalism student under a great teacher, Dr. David Manning White. I also owe a real debt of gratitude to the Boston University School of Theology, where, as a graduate student, I was permitted great freedom to study the relationship between preaching and communication. Particularly helpful to me were Dr. William Douglas and Dr. Allan Knight Chalmers of the School of Theology and Dean Melvin Brodshaug of the School of Public Communication. Dr. John L. Casteel and Dr. Reuel L. Howe also encouraged me in my research. Dr. Elton Trueblood has made some helpful comments on the manuscript for which I am deeply grateful. While they have all contributed to my thought, I am sure none of these men would care to be held responsible for my views.

My wife, Bonnie, has also been a great source of strength

and support during my pursuit of this matter, working full time while I studied at Boston University, then fending off the children, proof-reading, and brewing countless pots of coffee while I wrote this book. My friend Charles Johnston, among many, has given me much encouragement that I was on the right track. My competent secretary, Jim Bormann, has done his usual good job of improving on my manuscript while typing it, and his labors are much appreciated!

CLYDE REID

New York City
February, 1967

PROLOGUE

The Complacent Sower: A Parable

One fine morning a farmer set out to plant his field. He walked up and down with his seed bag at his waist, throwing the seed in a rhythmic motion with his head held high. He could feel the warm sun on his face as he walked.

"I love to watch the blue skies and the gentle clouds as I plant," he said to himself. "As I sow, I can dream of the great harvest to come. I can imagine the hungry children this crop will feed. I can see the workers who will earn their bread by the fruits of my labor. Surely, this is God's work!" Finally satisfied that he had sown enough, he went back to the farmhouse to think and wait. And the rains came and the sun shone on that field.

One week later, the farmer went again to his field and again he sowed a great deal of seed, walking up and down sowing to right and to left with his head held high looking at the clouds. Again he returned satisfied. "Surely, this is God's work," he murmured to himself. The other six days he spent sorting over his seed and studying the seed catalogues.

Again the next week, and every week that followed, he did the same, sowing great quantities of seed, then returning to the farmhouse to await the results.

When the end of the season had come, the farmer went to reap his harvest. But, alas, he had no crop to gather. The field was barren, except for a few scraggly stalks here and there and a great many weeds. The farmer was stunned. Where he had expected a great harvest, he found almost nothing. Angry and confused, he called in three experts to advise him.

"You men are authorities on planting and sowing. What has happened to my crop that I have no yield?"

The first expert spoke, "Well, it is obvious that you did not prepare the ground before planting. The earth was not plowed for the seed, and so it simply lay on top of the hard ground and did not put down roots."

The second man added, "Furthermore, you have sown far too much seed. The seeds have choked each other out. If you had sown less seed, those which you did sow might have had a better chance to grow."

The third said, "But even that is not enough. The field is too large for one man to work alone. Could you not train a crew of fellow workers to labor with you?"

"Gentlemen," he cried, "I thank you for your advice. You have been of great help to me." And so they went away.

The next spring, the farmer went again to his field, and walking up and down with his seed bag at his waist, he sowed his seed to right and to left in a lulling, rhythmic motion, his head held high and the warm sun on his face. A week later, he returned to his field and again sowed great quantities of seed. Week after week, he went to his field and sowed his seed. Often it was the same type of seed he had sown the week before, but sometimes it was a little different.

A friend stopped by one day and said, "Tell me, neighbor, why it is that you are sowing your field week after week and have paid no attention to the three experts who advised you so carefully?"

"Oh, those fellows!" he replied with contempt. "I'm sure they meant well. But not one of them is a farmer. Why should I listen to them?"

"But you had no harvest last year! And you are sowing this year's seed on top of last year's seed. Can you afford to go on like this year after year?"

"Look, friend," answered the farmer. "You can't tell me there will be no harvest. That is in God's hands alone, and his standards are not our standards. His ways are not our ways. Besides, I enjoy standing out here once a week in the warm sun with my head high sowing this seed. To be a farmer is to be a sower of seed. I find my occupation rewarding."

And so, year after year, he went on sowing his seed, claiming a great harvest, while his friends only shook their heads in bewilderment.

THE EMPTY PULPIT

I rarely hear a sermon I consider worth listening to.
                                                    —*A minister*

I listen just so long, and the sermon raises so many questions in my mind that I can't ask, that finally I quit listening and it just goes in one ear and out the other.
                                                    —*A judge*

He sits up there with a halo on top of his head and he can't speak to where I am—because we speak different languages.
                                                    —*A layman*

*Most congregations have no chance to express their minds, and so they sleep all through the sermon, lulled by the drone of our voices and by the unreal truisms we are mouthing.**
                                                    —*A priest*

When the preacher comes around, we put on a mask; we don't drink or do other things we'd like to do. And I'm sure he wears a mask, too.
                                                    —*A layman*

I am not immune to God: I am immune to Sunday morning.
                                                    —*A housewife*

The sermon makes us feel good, but it doesn't really change much.
                                                    —*A layman*

---

* Abbé G. Michonneau, *Revolution in a City Parish*. Westminster, Maryland: Newman Press, 1950.

Chapter I

THE PREACHING CRISIS

D on't preach at me!"

In using this common expression, we not only communicate a message but we express our view of preaching. For countless persons, preaching has become a word surrounded with negative feelings. We need to face this fact honestly and ask ourselves why this practice has gained such a reputation.

Preaching and preachers have been under attack for centuries. Today, however, the barrage seems to be growing in frequency and intensity. It may even be said that a cleavage is developing between those who are disillusioned with preaching as the primary mode of communicating the gospel and those who still defend preaching as the central act of the ministry. There are also those who are saying that the era of preaching is dead. It is my purpose in this chapter to set forth some of the charges being made against preaching today in order to get the problem squarely before us.

In his painfully honest manner, Pierre Berton, Canadian author and critic of the churches, has expressed how many persons outside the church feel about its preaching when he says that sermons today are "spiritless, irrelevant, dull, and badly delivered."[1] Many churchmen dismiss Berton's comments as the views of an outsider to the faith. "After all," they say, "if he is not himself a worshiping Christian, how can he be expected to enter into the spirit of what goes on in a service of worship?"

However, it is more difficult to dismiss a theologian like Helmut Thielicke when he writes that "preaching itself has decayed and disintegrated to the point where it is close to the stage of dying."[2] The first chapter of his book *The Trouble with the Church* is entitled "The Plight of Preaching." John W. Doberstein admitted in his foreword to Thielicke's book: "We are being told that the day of preaching is over and that it is a vain hope ever to revive it. . . . No one will quarrel with the facts about the state of preaching today; but we may well challenge the conclusion that is drawn."[3]

I have found many who do quarrel with the facts, who do not admit that preaching today is really in any trouble. My own experience, however, has been that of Berton and Thielicke. For four years, my work as a seminary field work supervisor took me into many churches of the major denominations. In the course of supervising a student's work, I often worshiped in the church where the student served as an assistant to the minister. I heard many sermons in churches of

[1] *The Comfortable Pew* (Philadelphia: J. B. Lippincott Company, 1965), pp. 96–97.
[2] *The Trouble with the Church.* Translated by John W. Doberstein (New York: Harper & Row, 1965), pp. 1–2.
[3] *Ibid.*, pp. vii–viii.

all sorts from wealthy suburban and status-metropolitan to poor inner-city congregations.

While I have deep respect for many of the ministers of those churches and the work they are doing, the sermons I heard were frequently weak. They tended, with exceptions of course, to be long, rambling, dry, uninteresting, and remote from the current realities of life in the twentieth century. I remember the Sunday following the passage in Congress of the great Civil Rights Bill of 1964. In my own spirit, I wanted to praise and glorify God in some act of thanksgiving for this step ahead in man's humanity to man. I worshiped that Sunday in one of the great Protestant churches in America, but I waited in vain for the ministers even to mention the passage of the bill, much less to offer praise and thanksgiving for it.

In all those sermons, I heard very few illustrations from the life experience of the preacher himself. In fact, I heard very few illustrations of any sort. The preacher tended to speak of vague ideas and concepts, but rarely put flesh on the ideas by illustrating them in terms that are meaningful to the average layman. On the whole, the sermons were poorly organized and poorly presented with very little clarity of theme. I often left completely in the dark as to the preacher's theme or message. I heard very little passion, very little conviction.

Further, I saw little difference in the life of the churches as a result of the preaching, and some of the coldest, most unfriendly churches I've ever attended have been those with the "greatest" preachers.

Apart from my own sermons (which tend to be interesting, stimulating, vital, and concise, of course), my experience with preaching on the whole has been discouraging. I almost dread enduring another sermon in fear that it will be as dreary as most I have heard lately.

In an article entitled "Is Preaching Outmoded?" Theodore O. Wedel has summarized some of the current debate on the preaching crisis. While Wedel's position is basically a defense of preaching, he cites some of the current criticisms. He quotes the president of a large eastern seminary as saying "Preaching is gone to pot," and cites a layman as saying "Many in our parish regard the pulpit as harmless and boring."[4]

Wedel quotes Eric Muller-Gangloff, a leader in the Academy Movement in Germany, as proposing that dialogue replace the sermon: "Many indications point to the end of the era of the sermon as primary agent of communicating the gospel. Why . . . may not open dialogue replace the sermon and classroom lecture?"[5] Wedel himself affirms the value of small group dialogue in the life of the church, but rejects the idea that dialogue should replace the sermon. Others who defend preaching are less generous and would dismiss dialogue in small groups as "the pooling of ignorance."

On every hand preaching is being questioned and criticized not only by those outside the church, but by those within who are concerned for the genuine communication of the gospel. Even Henry Sloane Coffin admitted, in 1952, that "there is much current disparagement of preaching, and that among some of the more thoughtful in our churches."[6] It is my opinion that the disparagement of preaching today is suffi-

4 In *Religion in Life* (Autumn, 1965), p. 534.
5 *Ibid.*, p. 537.
6 *Communion through Preaching* (New York: Charles Scribner's Sons, 1952), p. 2.

ciently serious to warrant very careful attention to the charges. As I read the current criticisms of preaching, they fall into at least seven distinct categories.

Charge #1—*Preachers tend to use complex, archaic language which the average person does not understand.* This is one of the most common complaints against preaching today. When the minister speaks of the "anthropomorphic God" or the "glory of redemption," he may have in mind some very powerful ideas. If these mental images or concepts are not shared by those to whom he is preaching, then communication has failed and he has repeated the great words in vain. As a young public relations executive once put it, "I wish our clergy would learn something about communication. They're up there talking a language all their own; you can't understand a word they say. It's boring! It's enough to put you to sleep."

As a student I once attended a service in the local congregation with a noted teacher of theology. I have not forgotten . . . what this professor said to me after listening to the utterly miserable sermon. "The first thing I do when I enter the church," he said, "is to look around and note with sadness that hardly one of my colleagues from the other faculties is sitting in the pews. But when the sermon is over, I usually say to myself: What a good thing that none of them was there!" He went on to say, "I do not demand that this harassed man in the pulpit give me a rhetorical treat or brilliant food for my interest. . . . But one thing I could well do without and that is the peculiar tone, the same old tune." He was referring to the usual criticism: the mere grinding out of a routine vocabulary—God, grace, sin, justification—which produces a kind of Christian gobbledegook that never gets under anybody's skin and at most elicits the reaction: Well, that's the way the minister has to speak, but what's it to me?[7]

7 Thielicke, *op. cit.*, pp. 2–3.

Charge #2—*Most sermons today are boring, dull, and uninteresting.* I recently attended the service of worship at a church which lists 2,100 members on its rolls. Of those 2,100 persons, about 100 were in attendance that Sunday. In other words, about one in twenty felt obliged to worship that week. It was a summer Sunday, but it is hardly conceivable that 95 per cent of the congregation could have been away on a given weekend. I am convinced that many of them stayed away because they do not find that the traditional, sermon-centered service of worship holds their interest. As one great pulpiteer has put it: "Surely, we preachers must have sadly muddled things! For we have, far and away, the most exciting and most glorious tale in the old world to tell, and it seems we have not fascinated and enthralled them with it, but so bored them that they can somehow keep from hearing it."[8]

Thielicke asks, "Have we not become unbelievable and unconvincing in our Christian preaching—not in the penultimate but in the ultimate dimension—because our preaching no longer reaches people, because it is boring and colorless?"[9] I once heard a famous preacher tell of the little lady who approached him after he had preached at a home for the aged. After some discussion, he admitted, "I'm afraid I preached too long." "Oh no," she replied, trying to reassure him, "it wasn't too long; it just seemed long." For whatever reasons, whether we like to admit it or not, many persons feel that preaching today fails to capture their interest. It is a charge we must take seriously.

[8] Arthur J. Gossip, *The Hero in Thy Soul* (New York: Charles Scribner's Sons, 1929), p. 150.
[9] *Op. cit.,* p. 18.

Charge #3—*Most preaching today is irrelevant.* The charge is often heard that preaching today does not reach the needs of modern man. People have difficulty seeing any direct connection between the words of the preacher and the day-to-day world in which they live and make their decisions. They may suspect that there is a connection, but the message is not presented in such a way that they can grasp that relevance.

Earl H. Furgeson has spoken of this failure to be relevant:

> Falling asleep during preaching is the symptom of failure in communication, for which the preacher as well as the listener may be responsible. When the meanings begin to blur, the listener's attention fades and, like a driver overcome by the monotony of the road, he gives up. Irrelevance, or the failure to convey significant meaning, is a prime factor. . . .[10]

One possible explanation is that the relevance exists in the preacher's mind, at a theoretical level. Although it may exist in the preacher's thought world, that meaning may never have been tested in actual behavior or experience, so he cannot put it into concrete action language. Thus the impact remains trapped in his idea language, the language of the theologian or philosopher, while most of his listeners live in a world of action language.

Whatever the underlying reasons for this failure to communicate, we need to accept the fact that many persons *feel* the irrelevance of preaching. *We* may believe the faith to be relevant, but our listeners are not being helped through preaching to grasp this relevance.

Charge #4—*Preaching today is not courageous preaching.* This charge may simply be an extension of the charge that

[10] "Abstractions in Preaching," *Pastoral Psychology* (October, 1963), p. 8.

preaching is not relevant. To be relevant in today's world of rapid change is necessarily to be challenging, upsetting, and disturbing at times, as well as inspiring and comforting at others. A steady diet of either challenge or comfort is a distortion of the gospel. But the temptation is often strong to comfort the afflicted rather than afflicting the comfortable.

I once asked a genial old preacher who had earned additional fame as a teacher of homiletics, "Has your preaching ever made your parishioners angry with you?" He looked shocked that I would ask such a question. "Oh, my no," he replied. I wondered how he could have preached the gospel and failed to disturb people some of the time. Harvey Cox has said it: "Our preaching today is powerless because it does not confront people with the new reality which has occurred and because the summons is issued in general rather than in specific terms."[11]

A common charge is the claim that the minister himself does not live a courageous life. Because he does not open himself to risk, his preaching cannot be genuinely courageous either. His actions do not communicate the realities of which he speaks on Sunday morning, and "actions speak louder than words."

It is this failure to speak the prophetic word with courage and power which must lie behind the all too common image we find in the mass media of the weak, frightened, harmless minister. While this "Milquetoast" image certainly applies to many clergymen, there are many others who belie the image and live courageous, sacrificial lives.

[11] *The Secular City* (New York: The Macmillan Company, 1965), p. 122.

Charge #5—*Preaching does not communicate.* I shall never forget spending an evening recently with an old friend who has been a lifelong churchman. A man who has established his reputation as a journalist, poet, and composer, he will soon retire from active professional life. It was not surprising during our evening together that the conversation turned to religion. At one point in the discussion, he looked me in the eye and asked, "What is God, anyway?" In all his years as an active member of a local Protestant church, this man had not been confronted with the reality of the Christian God, despite hundreds of sermons. It is personal encounters such as this which lend credence to the oft-repeated claim that preaching does not adequately communicate the content of the gospel.

This is one of the findings of Ronald J. Parsons in his recent doctoral research. Testing lay persons from a number of churches in the Detroit metropolitan area, Parsons found that "the intended content of the sermon is very poorly communicated."[12] He found that in meetings immediately following the worship service, *less than one-third* of the persons tested could give a reasonably clear statement of the primary "question" of the sermon or the "answer" suggested in the message. "The Church and sermons are experiencing widespread criticism for failing to communicate meaningfully in contemporary society," Parsons concluded.[13]

Another recent piece of research supports Parsons. Following the morning worship service in a New England church,

[12] "Lay Perception and Participation in the Communication of the Sermon." Unpublished Ph.D. dissertation, Boston University, 1966, p. 184.
[13] *Ibid.,* p. 217.

271 persons filled out questionnaires. Fifty-six per cent felt the minister's sermon was "superior" and another 35 per cent felt it was "good." However, only 21 per cent could reflect the minister's *central message* clearly and accurately, and 40 per cent omitted any reply at all when asked what that message had been.[14] *It causes one to wonder what it was that was "superior" when only one person in five could remember the central point of the sermon.*

In a recent book, Philip A. Anderson reminds his readers of the experience of Richard Baxter, a seventeenth-century English minister. Baxter had preached three times a week for twenty years, but found himself dissatisfied with the religious life of his congregation. When he began calling in their homes, he discovered how little his people had actually learned of the Christian faith from all his preaching. So Baxter began a program of regular visiting and teaching in their homes, meeting with the family around the kitchen table. He found that he often accomplished more in that one hour with the family than he had in years of preaching.[15]

Charge #6—*Preaching doesn't lead to change in persons.* Closely related is the charge, heard with some regularity, that preaching does not change persons. According to a recent issue of *Time* magazine on the racial crisis in the South, "many signs show that preaching alone is disappointingly ineffective. Chief among them is the segregation that still thrives within the church despite a striking increase in sermons on integration. . . ."[16] There are many other indica-

14 "A Study of the United Church of Christ, Plainville, Connecticut," Church Surveys, Boston University, August 4, 1964.

15 *Church Meetings That Matter* (Philadelphia: United Church Press, 1965), p. 10.

16 *Time*, Oct. 4, 1963, p. 80.

tions that the churches' deeds do not match their words from the pulpit, and that the churches are faced with a serious *integrity crisis* as a result.

A recent newspaper article illustrates one facet of this problem. It reads as follows:

> The views of Protestant and Roman Catholic churchgoers on issues such as the war in Vietnam and the speed of integration are almost identical with those of non-churchgoers, an official of the American Institute of Public Opinion stated today.
>
> George Gallup, Jr., managing director of the Institute, which is better known as the Gallup Poll, said that churchgoers tended to be "better informed, more socially involved, and happier than non-churchgoers."
>
> As a group, however, churchgoers are no more inclined than the population as a whole to be "doves" on the Vietnam issue or to become "crusaders" on issues such as capital punishment, Mr. Gallup reported.[17]

While this one report is not enough to prove that preaching does not change persons, it is disturbingly suggestive. If it makes no difference to be a Christian, then why go to church? If the followers of the Prince of Peace favor war as much as the nonbeliever, then in what ways are they unique?

Ross Snyder was touching on an aspect of this problem when he wrote that man learns in new ways in the new age. Man now learns by dialogue with others who have had experiences and ideas, rather than primarily by reading books. Snyder adds, "Preaching is a dead duck for him—except in the context of intense common fate."[18]

Charge #7—*Preaching has been overemphasized.* In 1964 a conference on communication was jointly sponsored

[17] *New York Times,* January 19, 1967.
[18] *The Ministry of Meaning* (World Council of Churches and World Council of Christian Education, 1961), p. 12.

by the Vanderbilt University Divinity School and the Office of Communication of the United Church of Christ. Conference delegates expressed their disillusionment with preaching and agreed that the traditional sermon was ʃone of the least satisfying methods for extending religion's message to out-ₗsiders." A news item reporting the conference began with this statement: "American Protestantism was said this week to have failed to communicate with the world around it because it depended too much on preaching and spoke in a language that was unintelligible to the man in the street."[19]

There are many today who are pointing to fresh new ways of communicating the gospel, and are saying, in effect, that we should not rely so heavily upon preaching any more. The emphasis on small groups in the life of the church, the experimental ministries carried on by urban ministers and night ministers, the coffee-house experiments, are all efforts to communicate with modern man through nonpreaching ministries. James B. Miller has written: "Without bringing into question for one moment the importance of public proclamation of the gospel from a Protestant pulpit, the fact remains that the task of the church as far as 'preaching' the gospel is concerned does not solely rest in a pulpit nor in the verbal efforts of a minister once a week."[20] Even Theodore Wedel has admitted that "the idolization of the sermon as possessing monopoly rights in the communication of the Christian faith needs dethronement."[21]

I recall vividly the occasion when an outstanding lady social

[19] *New York Times*, January 18, 1964.
[20] "Communicating the Gospel through Teaching," *Encounter*, XVIII (Autumn, 1957), p. 402.
[21] *Op. cit.*, p. 538.

scientist was meeting in seminar with a group of ministers. The subject of preaching came up. The lady, who has earned a wide reputation as an author and lecturer, leaned forward and addressed the clergymen with great clarity: "You see, you ministers have made preaching so terribly unacceptable."

If preaching has indeed become unacceptable, and if the formidable charges brought against it today are only half-true, then the problem deserves serious attention. It well behooves the church to raise the question as to whether the sermon is an adequate vehicle for the communication of the gospel in the new day. The rest of this book is an effort to do just that. I shall begin by summarizing the theological and practical arguments advanced in defense of preaching, then raise some further questions and outline some additional dimensions of the problem.

Chapter II

PREACHING DEFENDED

Despite the heavy barrage of attacks on preaching today, there are plenty of giants who rise to its defense at the slightest opportunity. Books are still pouring from the presses extolling the importance of preaching. Homiletics, the art of preparing and delivering sermons, is still a major course in every school of theology. New churches are still being built by the hundreds with the pulpit a prominent piece of furniture. Annual series of lectures on the virtues and devices of preaching are still offered in many places. "To downgrade the pulpit will be fatal," says John W. Doberstein. "With preaching Christianity stands or falls," quotes Wedel.

David A. MacLennan raises the question, "Is the pulpit and its preaching obsolete?" He answers with a ringing no, affirming that it has been the experience of the church that preaching is a "singularly effective means of grace" which God has ordained.[1] In the words of Paul M. Van Buren, at the center of the minister's work stands proclamation, "his weekly task of wrestling with the biblical witness to God's self-revelation until he can stand up on Sunday and proclaim the Christ of the apostles as Lord with such faithfulness to the biblical witness that his feeble words can truly become the word of God. . . ."[2] According to Van Buren, without the faithful proclamation of Christ, the church will wither and die.

Louis H. Gunneman expressed it well when he wrote: "The fact is, however, that preaching is the core means of realizing and making known God's presence and work. Abandon this occasion of personal confrontation, and worship soon must live on memory alone."[3]

A more dramatic expression of the central importance of preaching is found in the words of Arthur L. Teikmanis:

> If preaching were to cease, an unprecedented revolution would result which would affect not only the earth but also the sky and the planets. Parents would come to us and say, "You are taking away life's meaning and the faith of our children." Responsible citizens would complain, "You are undermining our morality, our social order, and our culture." . . . It is a necessary ingredient of genuine living.[4]

With such fervent defenses of preaching, it would be well to examine more closely the arguments advanced for assigning such a central place to the sermon.

[1] Entrusted with the Gospel (Philadelphia: Westminster Press, 1956), p. 26.
[2] "The New Biblical Theology in Parish Life," Religion in Life (Autumn, 1959), pp. 534–535.
[3] Worship (Boston: United Church Press, 1966), p. 31.
[4] Preaching and Pastoral Care (Englewood Cliffs: Prentice-Hall, 1964), p. 15.

WHAT IS PREACHING?

The word most commonly associated with preaching is *proclamation*. Preaching is the proclamation of good news, the news of what God has done in history for man, the good news of Jesus Christ. "Preaching tells of God's gift of life, which He gives to men through His Son Jesus Christ, who died on the cross and rose again that man might live."[5] The role of preaching is often defined as the proclamation of the Word of God. The same Word of God which became flesh in Jesus Christ, which is attested to in the Scriptures, is proclaimed through the sermon.

As Roy Pearson has put it, "The primary purpose of preaching is surely *proclamation*. . . . The gospel does not live unless it is proclaimed. . . . So the sermon is a proclamation. It tells what God has done in Christ. . . ."[6]

Beyond the element of proclaiming the good news of the Christian faith, a further claim is often made by theologians, namely, that in preaching the preacher's words become more than human. According to this view, his words are transformed and become something more. Walter Russell Bowie sounds both notes very clearly when he writes that the gospel is the proclamation of that which is incomparable. The life, death, and resurrection of Jesus Christ reveal the tragedy of human sin and the love of God. Furthermore, he adds, when the man who goes into the pulpit remembers that, then what he says there—even when his personal gifts are limited—has

[5] Richard R. Caemmerer, *Preaching for the Church* (St. Louis: Concordia Publishing House, 1959), p. 1.

[6] *The Ministry of Preaching* (New York: Harper & Row, 1959), pp. 15–17.

an exalted significance beyond all ordinary speech."[7] (Italics mine.) Leslie J. Tizard illustrates the same point when he says, "Preaching is not the activity of man alone; it is not merely a man who is speaking. God is speaking through him."[8] When a man is "really" preaching, he is an "inspired" man.

Christian theologians claim yet more for the sermon. For Emil Brunner, wherever there is true preaching and the Word of God is genuinely proclaimed, "in spite of all appearances to the contrary, the most important thing that ever happens upon this earth takes place."[9] James W. Clarke claims that preaching is not only the communication of the Christian gospel, but *"an integral part of the gospel itself."* Clarke claims that you cannot separate the gospel and the preacher. "You cannot have one without the other."[10] Clarke's view is perhaps the "highest" view of preaching expressed in the literature. For him, preaching is the supreme method of God's saving activity in history, though not the only method.

Langdon Gilkey also seems to hold a very high view of preaching. For him, Jesus Christ relates himself to the church as his community through the Word of God as it is preached, read, and responded to. We maintain our continuity with the church of the apostles by our faithfulness in preaching, teaching, and witness to the message of the early Christians as it is found in Scripture. He sees the minister's task as an awesome

[7] *Preaching* (Nashville: Abingdon Press, 1957), p. 17.

[8] *Preaching: The Art of Communication* (New York: Oxford University Press, 1959), p. 13.

[9] *Revelation and Reason* (Philadelphia: Westminster Press, 1946), p. 142.

[10] *Op. cit.*, p. 16.

one—to mediate the living Word to his congregation through his work as preacher, teacher, and pastor. Gilkey also stresses the crucial role of the Word being preached with relevance to the actual life of a specific congregation. His emphasis on the minister's task as the mediator of the Word would seem to place him with those who regard preaching as not only essential but an integral part of the Christian message.[11]

The Lutheran Caemmerer puts it this way: "Preaching does more than tell of this gift of life. It gives it. Through preaching God tells of His life to the world, but more: through preaching God gives Himself to the world."[12]

Pearson speaks of the sermon as a demonstration in which the Word of God is again made flesh in the preacher himself. According to Pearson, the minister experiences God as he preaches, and so the sermon becomes an event.[13]

So preaching is traditionally defined by one segment of Protestantism as the proclamation of God's good news in Jesus Christ, the life-giving Word of God, by a man whose words become more than human speech—whose words become God's saving activity incarnated in the present.

There are others who would assign preaching an important but not so exclusive role in the communication of God's saving grace. Rolland W. Schloerb feels it is sufficient to say that preaching remains an important part of the minister's task and therefore should be taken seriously.[14] Theodore Parker Ferris, one of America's great preachers, speaks of preaching as an important part of the Christian ministry, but

[11] *How the Church Can Minister to the World without Losing Itself* (New York: Harper & Row, 1964), pp. 74–103.
[12] *Op. cit.*, p. 1.
[13] *Op. cit.*, pp. 19–20.
[14] *The Preaching Ministry Today* (New York: Harper & Row, 1946), p. viii.

not the only part. While he speaks of preaching as a sacrament, he feels that the preaching ministry and pastoral ministry are closely related.[15] This view of preaching, which holds it to be one important element of the minister's task, undoubtedly represents a major stream of Protestant thought on the matter today, as does the "high" view of preaching I have just outlined.

THE PURPOSES OF PREACHING

Preaching has other purposes beyond proclamation and demonstration in Protestant thought, and we may examine a few of the more prominent views.

Leslie J. Tizard speaks of the aim of the preacher as trying to bring about "a personal encounter between God and the souls of his hearers." The preacher should lead men to meet God face-to-face in such a way that they cannot escape the impact of God upon their lives.[16]

A similar idea is well expressed by Wedel when he says that the sermon "contemporizes" the gospel, or brings it from the historical past into the now of human existence. "From a *then,* or 'once upon a time,' it confronts the hearer with a *now.*"[17] Pearson adds a dimension when he voices a familiar view: "Good preaching is always for a verdict," demanding a yes or no answer from the listener.[18]

For Pearson, the three primary purposes of the sermon are proclamation, demonstration, and *implantation.* He feels that

[15] *Go Tell the People* (New York: Charles Scribner's Sons, 1951), pp. 13–31.

[16] *Op. cit.,* p. 18.

[17] "Is Preaching Outmoded?" *Religion in Life* (Autumn, 1965), p. 545.

[18] *Op. cit.,* p. 24.

the sermon must justify itself in terms of its fruits. "A sermon seeks widened understanding, strengthened resolves, cleansed hearts, changed lives. . . ."[19] Pearson feels that if a sermon changes nothing, it has accomplished nothing. Schloerb sounds a similar note when he speaks of the aim of the sermon as not simply to provide new information, not to help them experience something they have not experienced before, but to "arouse them to take the next steps in their religious development. . . . Preaching is therefore a summons to action."[20] James W. Clarke also says that the purpose of the sermon is "to produce action."[21]

Another purpose of preaching often mentioned is simply that of inspiration. Surely a sermon has been worthwhile if it inspires men and women with the greatness and glory of God, or assures them of God's continuing presence and love.

With these multiple claims and affirmations plus many more, theologians today justify the minister's preaching role. They claim for it a long historical tradition rooted in the ministry of Jesus and his followers and clearly recorded in the scriptures. "Jesus Came Preaching," says George A. Buttrick in the title of a well-known book on sermonizing. How, then, do the theologians answer the criticisms of preaching today? It may be helpful to study some of their answers.

WHY, THEN . . . ?

If preaching is truly the proclamation of God's good news *and* the reenactment of the event of God's saving activity,

19 *Ibid.*, p. 23.
20 *Op. cit.*, p. 67.
21 *Op. cit.*, p. 18.

why, then, is preaching now in such ill repute? If preaching brings man face-to-face with God and makes the good news contemporary, why have the listeners not experienced the good news or come away convinced that they have seen God? If the goal of preaching is action, changed lives, why have sermons been so strongly criticized for failing to make a difference? Not many writers have addressed this problem directly, but several answers are commonly offered.

First, there are those who say that the problem with preaching today lies in the content of the message. We are simply not preaching the right message, they tell us, or men would respond differently. "Our sermons today are not biblical," is a familiar cry. "Sermons today deal with every whim and anxiety of man but do not begin and end with the content of the Bible; if only our preachers would stick to the Word of God, we could recover our lost faith."

Arthur Teikmanis feels that the popularity of religion in America has caused preachers to water down their message by eliminating the elements which might be offensive to the masses. "As a result," he says, "all preaching has been in disgrace. Very clearly, however, it is not preaching as such that needs to be thrown upon a scrap heap. We only need to be delivered from secular, unauthentic, and false preaching. True preaching is as indispensable as food and shelter and clothing, for no man can ever live by bread alone."[22] While Teikmanis may be right that Americans have watered down their prophetic preaching to please the crowds, we would require another explanation for the low reputation of the sermon in Europe, where churchgoing is not a popular sport.

[22] *Op. cit.*, pp. 14–15.

Another version of the answer that focuses on the content of the message is offered by Ferris. He feels that one reason so many sermons are ineffective is that they try to tell people what to do, not what they are, nagging people into being good rather than showing them goodness to attract them toward it. Ferris also emphasizes the importance of the sermon being communicated in language that is the language of the listener. He puts it cogently:

> When one examines the language of the average sermon that is preached today, one sees the reason why it is so unrevealing. The language is often the technical language of the theologian, language good in itself, which perhaps in an earlier generation laymen understood but which has long since lost its current usage. Theological language in a sermon is normally as out of place as botanical language is in a garden.[23]

A second answer often heard is that the problem with preaching today lies in the listeners. "There is nothing basically wrong with the preaching," according to this view, "but people are not really listening. They do not open their hearts to hear the gospel when it is proclaimed. They are too soft, too comfortable, too materialistic, and they do not want to hear the disturbing news of the Christian faith." While this view undoubtedly has some truth in it, few are offering it as the entire answer to the problem of weak preaching.

One of the most common answers advanced to explain poor preaching is the simple fact that the average minister does not spend enough time preparing his message. If only he would spend his mornings in his study struggling with the Scriptures and wrestling with ideas, so the argument goes, his sermons

[23] *Op. cit.,* pp. 28–29.

would be filled with power and relevance. Instead, the minister today spends his time on administration, reading his voluminous mail from denominational headquarters, attending committee meetings, and making pastoral calls. As a result, he has little time left to prepare his sermon, and tends to throw some ideas together on Saturday. If he expects to produce a stimulating message, he must be willing to discipline himself to long hours in the "homiletical workshop."

Thielicke, who has probably devoted more energy to analyzing the problem of today's preaching than any other theologian, offers a fourth answer. According to him, the problem lies primarily in the faith of the preacher. If the preacher himself does not live within the framework of the faith he proclaims from the pulpit, he will not be taken seriously. "What the preacher says in the pulpit must have a relationship to what fills the rest of his existence," says Thielicke. "If I see a breach, if I see no connection, between his Christian and his human existence—so argues the average person consciously or unconsciously—then I am inclined to accept the conclusion that he himself is not living in the house of his own preaching, but has settled down somewhere beside it, and that therefore the center of gravity of his life lies elsewhere."[24]

According to Thielicke, the way the minister talks about religion is one symptom of this integrity crisis. If the preacher talks about modern art and drama naturally, but speaks of religion in a special tone of voice as though it were something from another world, he reveals his separation of religion and life. He does not really do his thinking, feeling, and willing in

[24] *The Trouble with the Church*, pp. 5–6.

the same world as his world of faith. Thielicke emphasizes the
fact that this is a spiritual and theological problem.[25]

Ernest Fremont Tittle, some years ago, expressed the same
basic concern when he blamed the failure of preaching on a
lack of qualified preachers who practice their faith as well as
speak it.[26] Wedel, too, issues a plea for more courageous
preaching as the answer to the preaching dilemma today.
Wedel calls for more honest toil in the minister's workshop as
part of the answer, but suggests a fifth category in answer to
the problem when he writes: "Has it possibly been precisely
concern for the pulpit and the preacher in place of concern for
the gospel itself which has brought the ministry of preaching
to its present pass? When has popularity ever been the test of
the truth of God's Word?"[27]

PREACHING WILL PERSIST

It is with these arguments that most theologians today
defend preaching and urge its continuance. "So preaching
will persist," says George A. Buttrick after a dramatic defense of the preacher's role. "It is rooted in our seeking for
God and in His prior seeking of us. . . . All things change.
But the prophet abides. He is not of man: the sky opens to let
him through."[28]

It was in 1946 that James S. Stewart wrote in a similar
vein:

[25] *Ibid.*, p. 15.
[26] *The Foolishness of Preaching* (New York: Henry Holt and Company, 1930), pp. 301–314.
[27] *Op. cit.*, p. 546.
[28] *Jesus Came Preaching* (New York: Charles Scribner's Sons, 1936),
pp. 25–26.

Do not listen to the foolish talk which suggests that, for this twentieth century, the preaching of the Word is an anachronism, and that the pulpit, having served its purpose, must now be displaced by press or radio, discussion group or Brains Trust, and finally vanish from the scene. As long as God sets IIis image on the soul, and men are restless till they rest in Him, so long will the preacher's task persist, and his voice be heard through all the clamour of the world.[29]

It is perhaps not unfair to point out that most defenses of preaching consist of more preaching. They are impassioned, dramatic, sincere affirmations of what the writer feels about the role of preaching in the modern world. They rely very little on concrete evidence or research to support their claims, aside from an occasional reference to someone whose life has been changed dramatically by hearing a sermon.

There is also a disturbing tendency in some of the preaching literature to identify preaching and the Christian message as though they were one and the same. They seem to imply that if the minister cannot preach, he has no legitimate role or function to perform and the church will disappear.

It is my conviction that some of the crucial factors in the plight of preaching today are not adequately dealt with in most of the literature, if at all. These factors will be presented in the following chapter.

[29] *Heralds of God* (New York: Charles Scribner's Sons, 1946), p. 55.

Chapter III

THE NEW SITUATION

Where, then, does the truth lie? Is preaching sick unto death? Are we near the end of the preaching era? Or does the revival of preaching merely await preachers who are better trained and more courageous?

I confess that when I have read the latest defenders of preaching and studied their arguments, I am not satisfied with their answers. To affirm in a loud voice that preaching is here to stay is simply not enough. I must add a strong *however* to their arguments and point out that there are some deeper dimensions to the problem of preaching which we have not yet fairly confronted. Only when we have carefully studied the fact that we live in a new age, that we have an entirely new authority structure today, and that we live in a new communication structure—only when we have evaluated the implications of these elements can we begin to ask what the role of preaching is for the church today.

When all the defenses of preaching are in, when all the chips are on the table, there are too many questions unanswered. One might be stated thus: Why are there so few *good* preachers? Eugene E. Bartlett quotes a man who heard the great Phillips Brooks preach and referred to him as "a great water-main, attached to the everlasting reservoir of truth, and a stream of life pours through him by heavenly gravitation to refresh weary souls."[1] However, the same man made a startling contrast between Brooks and the average minister when he commented that most preachers "take to the pulpit a bucketful or half full of the Word of God and pump it out to the congregation."[2] When the great preacher is such a rare bird (now nearly extinct), why is it that the average congregation must listen week after week to a man who may have little gift for preaching, and endure his squeezing it out drop by drop? Why do we not sense more often the "exalted significance beyond all ordinary speech" of his words? As Norman Mailer once told an audience of Union Theological Seminary students and faculty in New York, "A sermon is a difficult art form, like a sonnet; maybe that's why there are so few good ones." Yet we expect every minister to pose as an artist week after prosaic week.

Here is another unanswered question:

How is it that people can hear *good* preaching all their lives and yet not know who or what God is? If the primary purpose of preaching is to proclaim what God has done in Christ, how is it that so few seem to get the message? A minister once preached a sermon on what he would do if he had a million

[1] *The Audacity of Preaching* (New York: Harper & Row, 1962), p. 23.
[2] *Ibid.*

dollars. Next day a wealthy parishioner appeared and gave him the million. Together they founded a new college. Illustrations like this are often used to justify preaching. But how often does it happen?

In a recent book on the parish, the author cites the instance of the World War I officer "indifferent to religion, who strayed into a London church and left the service a humble believer."[3] Certainly this happens occasionally. Nearly every minister I know can cite such an instance. But isn't it interesting that a preacher writing in 1964 must refer back to a World War I illustration to justify preaching? If preaching is God's supreme saving activity in history, why does that activity appear so powerless? If in preaching, God gives the gift of life to the world, why do we not receive it more often?

Again, if the purpose of preaching is to produce action, changed lives, why do we not see more fruits of that action? Let us assume that a large metropolitan church has an outstanding preacher, a man who knows theology and is well versed in the great issues of the day. Let us assume that he spends adequate time preparing his sermon, and does a decent job delivering it, and that the message is surrounded by a magnificent building and great music. And let us say that he has preached courageously on brotherhood, racial equality, and the need for the Christian to live for others.

Why is it that the slum owners warming the pews in that church do not improve their buildings to provide decent homes to those who pay them their rents? Why is it that the church itself spends more on keeping up its magnificent

[3] Browne Barr, *Parish Back Talk* (Nashville: Abingdon Press, 1964), p. 19.

structure than in ministering to the poor? Why is it that so few creative ventures to bring the gospel to the world around it flow from that church? Why are the churches with the finest preachers not the trail-breakers in new forms of ministry to the world so that we must look elsewhere for models of what it means to be a faithful Christian fellowship? If we claim, as we do, that *Christian action* is the goal of preaching, then why does not action issue forth more visibly where preaching is at its best? These are the questions the world is asking of us in the churches today, and they deserve better answers than we have yet given.

Francis O. Ayres has expressed the dilemma in these words:

> The church talks a great deal about God, but the world cannot see that he makes any difference. The church has exhausted the possibilities of propaganda. In the process, it has cheapened such words as preaching, mission, and gospel to the point where they are almost meaningless. If you doubt this, spend a Sunday listening to "religious broadcasts" sponsored both by the established denominations and by fringe sects. If you don't find yourself screaming: "Words, words, words. I'm so sick of words . . . Show me!"—well, you can listen again the following Sunday and have your reward.[4]

No, the problem of our preaching crisis today is not solved by better-trained, more courageous preachers working harder on the preparation of their theologically sound proclamations. Even when we have this, and we rarely do, it is not enough to make a difference. The problem is a much more pervasive one, and we are called to study the new situation in which we live in order to understand it.

[4] *The Ministry of the Laity* (Philadelphia: Westminster Press, 1962), pp. 134–135.

We Live in a New Age

In the summer of 1966, the *Saturday Review* published an excellent special issue on "The New Computerized Age." If it is still possible for you to doubt that we live in a new, technological space age, then I recommend that you read the articles in this issue. The editors begin by quoting Dr. Jerome B. Wiesner, Dean of Science at the Massachusetts Institute of Technology. Dr. Wiesner points out the far-reaching social consequences of the development of the computer, and adds, "We have actually entered a new era of evolutionary history, one in which rapid change is a dominant consequence. Our only hope is to understand the forces at work and to take advantage of the knowledge we find to guide the evolutionary process."[5]

The articles elaborate the problems and the potentialities of the automation revolution. From education to book translation, from industry to engineering, the computer with its vast ability to store and use information will bring radical changes. The total impact of reading this material is that every aspect of our lives will be affected by this new age. John Diebold said it most plainly: "If there is one salient fact about information technology, it is that it is going to produce enormous social change. As the quality of life is changed, as the rate of learning, information, travel, and communications all change, we will see a major change in living patterns, in hopes and desires. In short, a complete new environment will exist."[6]

[5] Issue of July 23, 1966, pp. 15–16.
[6] *Ibid.*, p. 18.

Interestingly, Diebold's article is entitled "The New World Coming." Another article in the same issue, written by David Sarnoff, is entitled "No Life Untouched." Those of us who hope to go on living in the past may find it increasingly difficult.

Illustrations of the new technological age in which we live could be multiplied. Two primary aspects of the new age deserve our attention because of their direct implications for understanding the preaching crisis.

The New Authority Structure

Writing in 1960, James W. Clarke commented that "taking all things into account, the true and able Christian preacher is still the most significant man in the community. . . ."[7] Half a century ago, Clarke's words would have been true of many communities in America. His words may still be true in a few protected pockets of American life. But it is precisely this authority structure which has changed. The minister is no longer the most significant man in the community; the atomic scientist, the engineer, the psychiatrist, and others now occupy more prestigious positions. We may believe that the minister should be at the top of the list, but in the eyes of the world it simply is not so. A number of contemporary writers have documented this shift in the authority pattern in our culture.

According to James H. Robinson, "the preacher once enjoyed a wide and uniquely central place in the life of our society. Time and progress have changed it radically. The

[7] *Dynamic Preaching, op. cit.,* p. 49.

place is still unique, but it is no longer central." Robinson went on in his 1955 Beecher lectures to point out the profoundly significant role the minister played in the early life of this country. He helped to shape the government, initiate schools, start hospitals. According to Robinson, the minister was the "cornerstone of the community." Within his lifetime, Robinson has seen this pattern change completely, and now admits that a host of skillful professionals carry out the functions once centered in the ministry.[8]

Leslie Tizard summarized the situation well when he wrote: "Many a minister now has to recognize that there is probably somebody who knows more about every subject than he does with the possible exception of divinity—and some of us cannot even be sure about that!"[9] One of the clearest statements of this new authority pattern was written by Theodore Wedel in his article, "Is Preaching Outmoded?":

Only a septuagenarian like myself, I presume, can appreciate fully what the arrival of our mass communication media (radio broadcasting alone is only a scarce forty years old) has done to the one-time pride of the pulpit. The preacher had rivals for audience attention in those earlier days also—the lyceum and chautauqua lecturer and the political campaign orator. But this rivalry was sporadic and threatened pulpit monopoly of the air waves only lightly. Those were the days of the gospel tent and the city tabernacle, of the charismatic evangelist, of the era, in both England and America, of the Great Preachers, such as Phillips Brooks, or Henry Ward Beecher, or Robertson of Brighton. That era is gone beyond recall, even though a Billy Graham is still a belated successor. If the fate of the gospel in our half of the twentieth century depends on the pulpit's regaining the splendor of the Victorian age, the renewal of the church is a vanishing dream.[10]

[8] *Adventurous Preaching* (Great Neck: Channel Press, 1956), pp. 19–20.
[9] *Preaching: The Art of Communication, op. cit.*, p. 30.
[10] *Op. cit.*, p. 536.

In his helpful book *Church Meetings that Matter*, Philip Anderson has mentioned an additional dimension of this authority structure problem. He points out that in the sixteenth, seventeenth, and eighteenth centuries, few people could read and there were no other opportunities for them to learn the news of the day. They relied heavily upon the gatherings of the church and the learning of the pastor to bring them news by word of mouth. This pattern has now changed drastically, and church gatherings are only one of many meetings in the community.[11]

The change in the authority accorded the minister has its parallel in the role of the teacher in our culture. In an interesting book published a few years ago by the National Education Association, there is a chapter entitled "The Changing Role of the Teacher." The chapter documents the shift in status experienced by the teacher in American life and discusses some of its implications. Half a century ago, the teacher was a commanding figure in the community by virtue of the knowledge which he possessed and which was shared by few others. "As a source of certain kinds of information he was without a peer. As a performer, he could be measured chiefly against other teachers and the town's preachers."[12] The teacher had the power to provide a view of a larger world that was "a novel and stimulating experience."

The report goes on to point out that today's teacher generally is better prepared than those of 1900, but "the social context within which he works has changed." The explanation follows:

[11] *Op. cit.*, pp. 9–10.
[12] *Mass Communication and Education* (Washington, D.C.: National Education Association of the United States, 1958), pp. 75 ff.

Through the mass media, a whole new set of prestige figures has arisen. The teacher's interpretations of political matters are overshadowed by a host of radio and television commentators; his discussions of the geography and customs of other countries are made pale by the polychrome eye of the motion-picture cameras; his standards of music are obliterated by . . . disc jockeys . . . his readings of Shakespeare are made amateurish by professional performance. In essence, among the chief changes in the circumstances of teaching brought about by the rise of the mass media has been the loss of the aura of authority.[13]

The minister has suffered a similar fate. Like the teacher, his isolation is gone, the competition for time, information, and entertainment is intense, and his competence even in his special area of expertise may be challenged by his listeners. The narrowed gap in both formal education and experience may be the most crucial factor in this changed authority structure. Many parishioners not only have bachelor's degrees and Ph.D.'s, but they have instant access to information from all over the world. As Dr. John Casteel, noted author and authority on church life, likes to put it, "How can he expect them to be sheep when so many of them have sheepskins?" In addition, many parishioners have traveled widely in America and abroad, and have had firsthand experience of the world at large which their minister may not have shared. Not too many ministers travel around the world on the salaries paid by churches.

One evening I met a man at the home of a friend. To my surprise, I learned that he was a member of the same congregation to which I belonged at the time. He was a national executive of an important organization and had traveled ex-

13 *Ibid.*, p. 76.

tensively in the Western Hemisphere. He had had opportunities to observe the Christian mission at work in some very interesting corners of the world. He almost certainly knew more about the overseas work of our church than did the minister of the church, and from personal experience. So far as I know, he has never been asked to share this knowledge with the congregation. Should we wonder that he does not choose to attend regularly and listen passively when he is never permitted to share from his rich store of experience? I am confident that his example is multiplied over and over in our churches across the land.

There is at least one additional dimension of the new authority structure which is worthy of mention. The average parishioner is learning that what he thinks and believes is important. Because of enlightened personnel practices, his views make a difference on the job; higher levels of management grant him the right to share in decisions. His point of view is considered valuable in many of the organizations to which he belongs because of widespread use of group dynamics insights. He is learning by experience that *his authority* is worth something, and that he need not sit in abject dependence upon his superiors in many areas of his life. He can now contribute, speak and be listened to, and make a difference to others who share his life. He is learning to participate meaningfully in his world.

The church, unfortunately, has been moving slowly toward this new, participative authority structure. The time-honored tradition of a group of dependent listeners sitting mutely week after week at the feet of the clergy with no chance to participate in a meaningful way is now becoming a stone around our necks. The man who has ideas and can contribute them meaningfully on the job, at the club, and in his professional organization becomes increasingly restless with the role of silent listener. A highly intelligent mother was expressing this impatience with her church when she said, "Isn't it strange that I always have to be audience?" Another layman voiced the same concern: "The church sees my role as filling up a seat. I now know I'm worth more than that!"[14]

We live in a new authority structure, and the minister no longer can command a hearing simply on the basis of his being a minister. People do not listen to his words as they once did, and we must adjust to this new life situation. The minister now needs to discover his new role, and this is probably all to the good.

The report on the role of the American teacher shows what the teacher must now be willing to face. "More than ever, today's teacher cannot afford to be dull; the challenge to his inventiveness and enthusiasm is very great."[15] Furthermore, the teacher's new role offers him many advantages the teacher of 1900 did not have. He now has new tools and new knowledge that can make teaching more effective. He is released from some of the routine duties and freed to work more with individuals. Even though he has lost some of his status, *he may be a better teacher*. "The real result, therefore, of the changed role of the teacher may well be to raise his activity to a new level of professional significance."[16]

Exactly the same opportunity is awaiting the minister. Even though he does not have the status he once had as *the*

---

[14] I am indebted to Elton Trueblood for these quotations.
[15] *Mass Communication and Education*, p. 77.
[16] *Ibid.*, p. 100.

authority in the community, new doors may open for him to minister to the needs of his people. James Robinson was pointing to one of these new possibilities when he wrote that it is not a discredit to the preacher that trained professionals now do many of the tasks he once did, and do them better. Robinson says we should be grateful to God that there are others to share the burden. "The preacher can have more time today to devote himself to the special task to which God has called him. Sooner than later, even the specialist will seek the minister either for help on the moral problem of his own life, or for cooperation on the larger moral problems of society."[17]

Preaching emerged in a time when the authority structure was vastly different. We must be willing to restudy our mode of communicating the gospel in the light of this new authority situation. The old pattern is no longer sufficient.

The New Communication Structure

Not only has the old authority structure which supported the preaching pattern vanished, but the minister must now speak to a *new man* as well. If he were simply competing with some new media of communication like radio and television, it would not be so complex. Some ministers speak as though this were the case. However, the problem is not that simple. Radio and television have changed things drastically. Man now learns, feels, and thinks differently than he did before the advent of electronic communication.

The writing and thought of Marshall McLuhan have helped to call attention to this new communication structure.

[17] *Op. cit.*, p. 21.

According to McLuhan, the medium of the printed word had a vast influence on the way men thought. As Erik Barnouw has summarized it so well, "He tells us that as print became the main cultural transmission belt for one generation after another, knowledge and ideas were necessarily processed into a linear, one-step-at-a-time form required by the medium. Man was thus pushed into sequential habits of thinking, quite unlike the complexity and richness and all-at-onceness of face-to-face communication, and without the resonance of the human voice."[18] Or to put it in other language, the form by which we absorb knowledge, in this case through the printed word, has an unconscious influence on the way we organize our thinking and how we perceive truth.

Now we live in an era in which our children grow up with the omnipresent eye of the television set intruding itself upon their lives. From their earliest days, they are being bombarded with electronic communication, and this cannot help but influence their mode of responding to the world. Speaking of McLuhan, Barnouw writes: "The core of his message is a persuasive idea. It is that each new medium [i.e. television] alters our psychic environment, imposing on us a particular pattern of perceiving and thinking that controls us to an extent we scarcely suspect."[19] McLuhan himself wrote that "the effects of technology do not occur at the level of opinions and concepts, but alter sense ratios or patterns of perception steadily and without any resistance."[20] According to McLuhan, "we become what we behold."

[18] "McLuhanism Reconsidered," *Saturday Review*, July 23, 1966, p. 19.

[19] *Ibid.*

[20] *Understanding Media: The Extensions of Man* (New York: McGraw-Hill Book Company, 1964), p. 18.

As early as 1961, Ross Snyder wrote in his book, *The Ministry of Meaning*, that "we are in the formative period of a new era of man." Snyder's description of the new communication structure is brilliant:

A new species of man is being produced by the history of our time and the revolution in communications. A new way of sensing life and growing meanings, of organizing life world, of being-in-the-world has come with electronic communication. A *new mode of human consciousness* is arising. We need to operate within it, and minister to it.

As contrasted with the consciousness produced by the printed page, by realistic face-to-face communication, and by first-hand experiencing, man will become increasingly a new type of mind. Any emergence of significant meaning will now happen within this new consciousness.[21]

Snyder goes on to point out that "abstract marks on a piece of paper" are no longer a primary source of truth. Wisdom now comes, according to Snyder, with seeing-hearing. It comes through all the senses at once rather than through abstractions. "The proto-plasmic nuclei of the brain are all quivering, intermingling in a web that ceaselessly is in motion. Sight, sound, movement, texture are simultaneous and globe-shaped. The brain finally becomes equipped to handle only diffuse, ambiguous wholes, instead of precise articulations."[22]

I recently visited the Museum of Modern Art in New York City and joined a group gathered around a large, dark opaque object. Suddenly the darkness gave way to brilliant color and shimmering movement. The combination of moving parts and changing color from electric lights within the "sculpture" was fascinating to watch. This new development in art symbolizes a movement away from "flat" or static art which appeals to the

[21] *Op. cit.*, pp. 9–10.
[22] *Ibid.*

viewer in one dimension only. The trend is toward art which reaches the viewer through several appeals at once. To this extent, it is a parable of the new age and of communication which is more alive and vital.

We cannot yet see the full impact of this newly emerging man with his new modes of perceiving truth. We do not yet know fully what it means for preaching. It certainly means that we cannot continue as before, for there are many signs that people do not *hear* preaching anymore, and particularly do not *hear* it in such a way as to influence their behavior at deep levels.

I will try to suggest a few of the implications of the "new age" and the "new man" which thinkers like McLuhan and Snyder are pointing to, even though (admittedly) it is a risky business:

1. We must find means of communication that will reach people "through all the senses at once." Just as the "happening" is replacing the street-corner orator, so we must find more involving modes to communicate what has happened to us by the grace of God. The repetition of words and abstractions from a pulpit on Sunday morning is not enough. We hear the echo, "Words, words, words. I'm so sick of words . . . Show me!"[23]

2. We must use a variety of methods to communicate to modern man, alternating our approach to reach him in different ways. To use the same rigid style of communication over and over, whether it be preaching or any other, is deadening.

3. Modern man will learn much more through actual experiences than through hearing speeches, logical proposi-

[23] Ayres, *op. cit.*, p. 135.

tions, or doctrinal formulations. For him, truth is much more a matter of total awareness than clear, logical ideas. We must learn to teach through involving him in action rather than talking at him when he has ceased to listen.

4. Modern man will be convinced more easily when our actions and deeds show a high correlation, when they do not contradict each other. It is hard to believe the person who says he is a man of peace but goes on beating his neighbor over the head. Modern man is quick to smell out the contradictions between our words and our deeds, and eager to point them out to us. The current insistence of our youth generation for integrity and an end to "phoniness" is an example of this new pressure for honesty.

5. The "new man" is increasingly impatient with those structures in which he is only a passive spectator. He wants *his* gifts to be recognized and honored as well as those of his leaders. He wants to be regarded as a partner rather than as a dependent follower, and he desires an increasing share in the decision-making processes which affect his life. Black power is an expression of this urge on a political level. I recently heard a man say that he will not attend any more meetings in which he is powerless, in which he knows in advance that nothing will happen. This is an expression of the same feeling on an individual level. Those communication structures which emphasize passive-dependent listening will continue to appeal to those who have strong needs to surrender their individuality to a father-figure. Those persons who have learned to trust their ability to think for themselves will be drawn to communication structures which honor their gifts—in or out of the church.

As Marshall McLuhan has put it, "The need for dialogue is a mounting one in the TV generation. They cannot accept any diminution of their adult status. To be treated as anything less than adult affects them with all the indignity of racial segregation."[24]

In addition to the problems posed by our new authority and social structures, we also know more about the nature of communication than we did fifteen years ago. We will now explore some of the implications of this new knowledge.

[24] "What TV Is Really Doing to Your Children," *Family Circle,* March, 1967.

Chapter IV

UNDERSTANDING COMMUNICATION

The task of the Christian churches is often described as that of communicating the good news of Jesus Christ. In most Protestant churches, the sermon is the tool most heavily relied upon to communicate the gospel, and surveys indicate that ministers see their preaching role as their most important function. It follows logically that Christians should be deeply interested in understanding the nature of communication.

Research into the communication process has become widespread in recent years. Since World War II, a dozen sciences have focused attention on this problem. The fields of mathematics, semantics, psychology, cybernetics, journalism, linguistics, small group psychology, psychiatry, and many others have provided research data. Some basic principles of communication are now emerging from a number of directions, and in this chapter we will examine a few of these important insights.

What is communication? It is helpful to remember that the word is based on the Latin *communis*, which means common. A leading researcher in the field of mass communication, Wilbur Schramm, has said that "when we communicate, we are trying to establish a 'commonness' with someone. That is, we are trying to share information, an idea, or an attitude. . . ."[1] When we speak of communicating the gospel, then, we are speaking of the effort to establish a commonness with someone in regard to the Christian faith.

Another helpful definition is that used by researchers at Yale University, who define communication as "the process by which an individual (the communicator) transmits stimuli (usually verbal) to modify the behavior of other individuals (the audience)."[2]

COMMUNICATION AS DIALOGUE

Until about 1950, researchers thought of communication chiefly as a simple, one-way process. In this more primitive conception it was assumed that when a communicator transmitted a message to an audience, it had basically the intended effect. This approach was described by the widely used formula, *"who* says *what* to *whom* with what *effect."*

Since 1950, however, there has been an increasing tendency to regard communication as a more complex, dynamic two-way relationship, modified by many situational factors, including primary group relationships, opinion leaders, and

[1] "Procedures and Effects of Mass Communication," *Mass Media and Education,* ed. Nelson B. Henry (Chicago: University of Chicago Press, 1954), p. 113.
[2] Carl I. Hovland, Irving L. Janis and Harold H. Kelley, *Communication and Persuasion* (New Haven: Yale University Press, 1953), p. 12.

other variables. This tendency to understand communication as a two-way process was spurred on by some of Kurt Lewin's research. In a volume published in 1947, Lewin reported on some highly significant experiments in achieving social change.

In the Lewin experiments, groups of women were used as subjects. Three groups were given lectures on the value of using beef hearts, sweetbreads, and kidneys as meats for the family table. The nutritious value of these foods was emphasized. Three similar groups were given the same basic information, but were allowed opportunity for group discussion about the issue. The results showed that only 3 per cent of the women who were in the lecture groups served one of the recommended meats. In contrast, 32 per cent of the women in the groups which included discussion, or two-way communication, served at least one of the meats.[3] Lewin concluded that "lecturing is a procedure by which the audience is chiefly passive. The discussion, if conducted correctly, is likely to lead to a much higher degree of involvement."[4] Later researchers have repeated this type of experiment in other settings, and found basically the same result. Group decision, in which there is opportunity for a two-way flow of communication, is more effective than the formal lecture in overcoming resistance to change in behavior.[5]

By the early 1950's, researchers were reporting studies stressing the value of feedback in communication. When

[3] Lewin, "Group Decision and Social Change," *Readings in Social Psychology*, ed. Theodore M. Newcomb and Eugene L. Hartley (New York: Henry Holt and Company, 1947), pp. 334–335.

[4] *Ibid.*

[5] Jacob Levine and John Butler, "Lecture vs. Group Decision in Changing Behavior," *Journal of Applied Psychology*, XXXVI (February, 1952), pp. 32–33.

members of a group were allowed to ask questions and discuss, they were able to solve problems with greater accuracy than when the leader did all the talking. Wilbur Schramm discussed the meaning of feedback in personal communication: "Consider what happens in a conversation between two people. One is constantly communicating back to the other. . . . The return process is called *feedback,* and plays a very important part in communication because it tells us how our messages are being interpreted."[6]

Perhaps the most important single statement in the literature summarizing the transition to the new view of communication was this statement by psychologist Franklin Fearing. The writer was speaking of the concern educators have for the violence and crime content on radio and television:

> This is understandable if we assume a simple causal relationship between the content of the communication and its effect, with the implication that the content, especially via the mass media, is accepted primarily on its own terms. Such an assumption we may call the "one-way" or "transmission-belt" theory of communication. In bald form it asserts that ideas are embodied in communications content by communicators and may be transmitted relatively intact to potential recipients.
>
> A different theory, and one much closer to the findings of research, may be called the "two-way" theory of communication.[7]

It is interesting to note that religious writers began speaking of the importance of two-way communication, or dialogue, at about this same time. The Jewish scholar, Martin Buber,

[6] Schramm, ed., *The Process and Effects of Mass Communication* (Urbana, Ill.: University of Illinois Press, 1955), pp. 8–9.

[7] "Social Impact of the Mass Media of Communication," in *Mass Media and Education,* ed. Nelson B. Henry (Chicago: University of Chicago Press, 1954), p. 172.

published his *Between Man and Man* in 1947. Buber places great stress on the problem of communication, and says that all genuine communication is dialogic, where there is a deep exchange of meaning between the parties. Among the writers who reveal Buber's influence, Lewis J. Sherrill and Reuel L. Howe stand out. Sherrill has written that when deep communication is taking place in the Christian community, "there is a profound encounter between self and self within a field of concern in which God . . . is participant. And this is a two-way current, because in deep communication all parties to the encounter are called out and drawn forth, while at the same time all parties to the encounter go forth out of themselves."[8]

Sherrill speaks of one-way communication as communication by pressure. He contrasts this with two-way communication in which there is a two-way flow between two or more persons. *It is improbable, Sherrill suggests, that an encounter with God can result from one-way communication about God in which one person exerts pressure to get another to respond in a certain way.* He also suggests that in true two-way communication, "something happens" which allows the grace of God to operate. Sherrill feels that dialogue or two-way communication is desperately needed in the world today.

Levels of Communication

One of the most crucial developments in the field of communication research in recent years is the tendency to distinguish a number of steps in the communication process.

[8] *The Gift of Power* (New York: The Macmillan Company, 1955), pp. 85–86.

In an important volume published in 1958, DeFleur and Larsen commented on this development:

. . . there must be some observable response before the communicative act can be said to result in some degree of communication. This is important because it helps to distinguish between "contact" and "communication." Interhuman communication can occur only when there is contact or exposure to a set of symbols. The ultimate in communication is only achieved, however, when the interacting parties understand each other, can identify with each other's point of view, and a transfer of meaning has taken place that influences conduct. A transition to this distinction between contact and communication in the mass media field is now occurring.[9]

This distinction between simple contact and communication which influences conduct is consistent with our current understanding of preaching. Preaching is often referred to as a "summons to action" or an effort to change lives. For this reason, the distinction between contact and communication is crucially important to our examination of preaching. Building upon the work of De Fleur and Larsen, my own effort to integrate current insights and research yields the following seven phases or steps in the communication process:

1. *Transmission* occurs when the communicator presents his message (or delivers his sermon). This is the first and necessary step, but if a radio announcer is transmitting his message and no one is tuned in to that station, no communication occurs. Far too often, we have assumed that when we broadcast or transmit our message, communication occurs. We do not realize that this is a naïve assumption. Even in a Sunday service, where people are looking at the commu-

[9] Melvin L. DeFleur and Otto N. Larsen, *The Flow of Information: An Experiment in Mass Communication* (New York: Harper & Row, 1958), pp. 22–23.

nicator as he speaks, they may not be listening. Their attention may be elsewhere.

2. *Contact* occurs when a listener has heard the message. Even though a person may appear to be listening to our sermon, we do not really know if we have established contact unless he reflects back to us in some way that he has heard. It is also true that we listen at many levels of our being. We can listen superficially while our minds race on at some other more important task, or we can listen with deep absorption. Without contact at some level there is no communication, for the message is not even heard.

3. *Feedback* is the return process by which the listener reflects information to the original communicator. Feedback is the third step in the process because it is nearly always a requirement if communication is to proceed beyond contact to the deeper levels leading to complete communication. When the listener is allowed to ask a question, make a comment, or otherwise express himself concerning the content of the message, feedback is established and there is a potentiality for dialogue. This also assumes that the original communicator is listening attentively for the feedback. A minister may be as superficial with his acceptance of genuine feedback as parishioners are with their "I enjoyed your sermon" type of comments.

4. *Comprehension* occurs when the listener genuinely understands what it is the communicator means by the message he has transmitted. Many persons hear sermons week after week which they do not understand. They have no opportunity for feedback to clarify the meanings, and so they go away acting as if they understand when they do not. They

do not want to reveal their inability to understand the minister's language; they do not want to feel more inferior than they already do, so they go away unenlightened. It is theoretically possible for comprehension to occur without the introduction of feedback, and it surely happens at times. It happens especially if the communicator is very clear and communicates in language which the listener understands. However, the chances for communication to reach the level of comprehension are greatly heightened when some feedback process is used.

5. *Acceptance.* It is possible for a person to both hear and understand the intended message of the communicator, but to reject it completely. Once he genuinely understands the message, he is in a position to accept it, ignore it, or reject it. One of the difficulties with any form of one-way communication is that the communicator does not know when his listener has rejected his message. Nor does he know the basis of that rejection, for which he may have an answer.

The problem is much more complex. We now know from recent research that the way in which an individual hears and responds to a message is influenced by his primary group relationships. Once the idea is clarified in his mind, he must decide if it conflicts with his standing in those groups which he considers important. If he hears a sermon on the evils of smoking, but belongs to a street-corner gang in which smoking is an accepted norm, he must balance his feelings about belonging to the gang with the message on smoking. His primary group relationships may be in the home, the office, or the club, or all three! They tend to influence the norms which regulate his behavior, but these primary relationships are rarely rooted in his church. A primary group tends to be an informal grouping of persons who keep in close touch with one another and communicate with one another face to face.

6. *Internalization.* Even if the listener has accepted the message, it may be at a superficial level. It may not influence his way of behaving. For example, a church member may hear a sermon on the moral obligation of a Christian to support racial integration. He may weigh this message against his primary group norms and decide that he can accept the preacher's message as his own. At the same time, he may go on behaving as before—ignoring Negroes, avoiding social contact with them, and throwing off signals of rejection when in their presence. The message has not become internalized so that it has really become his own and he has begun to act on the basis of its content.

7. *Action.* Researchers now tend to regard communication as incomplete unless it has reached the point at which the communicator and listener have a common, shared understanding and are *acting* on the basis of this understanding. "A transfer of meaning has taken place which influences conduct."

These seven stages may be represented in the following diagram. The circles represent persons, with the original communicator on the left. The two individuals come closer together symbolically as communication develops, until they act on the basis of some shared meaning. The arrows represent a message being sent. The tiny circles at stage four indicate the possible influence of primary group relationships. In actuality, these relationships are probably operative at all seven stages of communication.

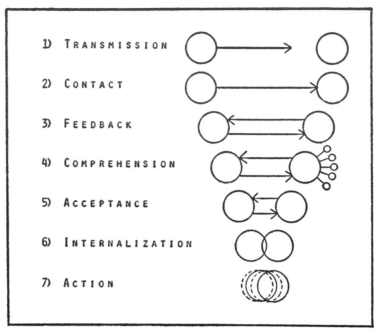

1) TRANSMISSION

2) CONTACT

3) FEEDBACK

4) COMPREHENSION

5) ACCEPTANCE

6) INTERNALIZATION

7) ACTION

—Diagram by Jim Bormann

This recognition of levels in the communication process, however they are spelled out, is of great importance for the communication of the gospel. If we really believe that the end product of Christian faith should be changed lives, in which persons behave differently toward each other, then we must be concerned about the completion of the seven stages just outlined. If we really believe that the goal of preaching is action, then we must develop processes which move us beyond mere contact to the deeper levels of communication.

Several points should be noted. There is nothing sacred about these distinctions as separate stages. Different terms could be used, and probably any one of these levels could be elaborated into additional steps. It is also possible for any particular communication event to skip stages, accomplishing complete communication without feedback, for example. The important point is that research increasingly points to the need for feedback or two-way communication in those instances when we expect comprehension, acceptance, internalization, and action to take place. To establish complete communication, monologue is rarely enough, and a two-way flow of communication is almost essential.

Edmund A. Steimle, editor of a recent book, *Renewal in the Pulpit*, suggests that there are signs of renewal in preaching. To demonstrate the truth of his thesis, Steimle offers a collection of outstanding sermons by young Lutheran pastors, nearly all of whom are now teaching in seminaries and colleges.[10]

There may well be some renewal in preaching, but we do not know that from the evidence Steimle has provided. All we know from his collection of sermons is that *some good sermon manuscripts are being written* by leading Lutheran clergymen. We do not know that these sermons were well delivered, nor that anyone *heard* them, much less understood them, accepted them, internalized them, or acted upon their message. We do not know if they were shouted in a holy tone or mumbled under the preacher's breath.

In short, we do not know from reading a manuscript that any communication took place whatsoever! We must now insist that our pastors and theologians become sophisticated about the nature of communication. This knowledge is wide-

[10] Philadelphia: Fortress Press, 1966.

spread in the world, and the churches cannot ignore it any longer.

Communication Integrity

While the principle of communication integrity is more an insight than a research finding, it is nonetheless important for the church. This insight has probably emerged from psychiatry and counseling, though it is also a concern to others. It may be summarized as follows: "The sum total of one's words and deeds constitute a message. When there is an inner contradiction between words and deeds, the deeds tend to communicate much more effectively than the words."

If a man strikes his fist on his desk, and says with red face and grim looks, "I am not angry," we tend to believe his actions rather than his words. We tend to adjust our response to him, taking his anger into account, even though he has just told us that he is not angry. Communication integrity must take into account the nonverbal communication of feelings and actions as well as verbal proclamations.

A minister may preach on the necessity of every Christian to be a man of prayer. At the same time, he may place all his program emphasis on other matters. He may never get around to training people in prayer techniques. He may never speak of prayer as a resource to those who come to him for help. He may never find time to pray himself. He may even discourage those who express interest in starting a prayer group. He is communicating one thing by his words, and another by his deeds. Why should he be shocked to learn that his parishioners are not men of prayer as he has advised them they should be? The integrity of his communication has been undermined by his deeds—consciously or unconsciously.

A church in a changing neighborhood decides that it will revive itself and launch a ministry to the poor now crowding its doorsteps. So the members rally around and raise some money to launch the new era of ministry. Their first expenditures are to repair the pipe organ and spruce up the stained-glass windows at a cost of eighty thousand dollars. The poor do not batter down the doors to get in, and the church is puzzled. "Why don't they respond to our efforts to reach them?" Again, our deeds communicate more loudly than our words, and to invite the poor into our upper middle-class sanctuaries will hardly convince them of our interest. When church members spend millions on themselves and devote a pittance to others, it is a little difficult to believe that they are "God's servant people."

People will have difficulty hearing our preaching so long as our deeds contradict the affirmations of our words from the pulpit. We need a deeply honest interior dialogue in our churches to help each other recognize the points where our communication integrity breaks down.

THE SERMON IS A MESSAGE

One of Marshall McLuhan's basic concepts—the medium is the message—may be applied to the sermon. As indicated in Chapter III, McLuhan tells us that every medium of communication has human effects quite apart from the intellectual content of the messages being sent by way of that medium. He speaks of the pervasive influence of television on how we think and act, aside from the actual programs we watch.

I will not attempt to summarize the richness and complexity of McLuhan's propositions here. Rather, I would like to call attention to a consideration of the sermon as a medium of communication. The sermon itself, apart from the content of its ideas or the feelings expressed, is a message. Furthermore, the context of the sermon—the pulpit, the ceremonies, the preacher's garb—modifies the message of the medium or adds to it.

Walk with me into one of the early New England Congregational churches. Here in the center of this church is an expensively carved pulpit in dark wood towering over everything else in the room. To enter it, the preacher must open a small door and climb a narrow stairway which winds up to the platform from which he speaks. Before ever the minister has opened his mouth, this pulpit has communicated a message.

The meaning of that pulpit has several aspects. One is that of authority. It proclaims loudly that the minister is not as other men. He is another sort of being, and no ordinary mortal should dare to stand as high. He is, as the cliché goes, "six feet above contradiction." This information proclaimed by the pulpit as a piece of furniture is consistent with the authority image of the preacher in colonial New England. He was probably without peer as the educated man in many communities, the dispenser of news, the interpreter of events, the newspaper, editorial page, and television eye rolled into one. Is this still the message we wish to communicate?

The pulpit as furniture proclaims another fact with theological roots. It says that the clergy are different from laymen.

The clergy are somehow God's special people, and laymen are to sit patiently and passively at their feet. They are to sit in awe and *look up* to the clergyman. This stands in direct contradiction to the words spoken from many of those pulpits today—that all Christians are God's servants and ministers. This new emphasis on the ministry of the laity may be puzzling to those who "hear" the message of the pulpit, which proclaims that the church's ministry is centered and focused in one man.

When the minister wears flowing robes into the pulpit, capped off by the brilliant colors of an academic hood, this communicates that the minister is religiously superior to ordinary persons.

The sermon itself bears a message apart from its ideas. Even where the physical pulpit is not as imposing as the old center pulpit of the traditional New England church, the sermon communicates some of the same information. The sermon structure ordinarily means that one man preaches, and all others in the congregation are expected to attend regularly and listen. One theme which this structure communicates very clearly is that of *dependence*. Laymen are to sit passively in a subordinate role to that of the preacher. Dependence is basically appropriate to the relationship between parent and child, or teacher and pupil, or doctor and patient. It may now be questioned whether dependence is appropriate to the minister-layman relationship on a permanent basis. If we really believe that every Christian is a minister, some new understanding must emerge, and we must begin to take seriously the contradictions in our verbal communication and the message of our deeds, including our preaching deeds.

COMMUNICATION DYSFUNCTIONS

Another aspect of the sermon as a medium lies in its *authoritarian* nature. Preaching is a one-way process, except in those rare situations when the minister has built in structures which involve him in a dialogue with his people. Basically, as it is generally practiced, preaching is a monologue by one man directed at his congregation. The listener has no opportunity to express his doubts or disagreements to the assembled group. He may even know factually that the preacher is wrong about some of the statements he makes in his monologue. An authoritarian structure is one in which power is focused in the leader, and preaching may be thought of in this sense.

The sermon structure, or the sermon as a medium of communication, proclaims that one man has the truth, the answers, and the insights. It also proclaims the reverse—that the man in the pew does not have truth, answers, and insights to share with the congregation. Preaching tends, therefore, to be a closed system in which the listener is expected to accept the message of the preacher as presented. Little room is left for his participation in the communication process. His involvement, therefore, tends to be minimal. He is not allowed to bring *his* truth to the event, but must accept another man's truth as final.

While the preaching structure may be communicating this "closed system" message, the preacher may be telling his people that he does not have all the answers. He may be telling them in good liberal style that they must wrestle with the Christian faith and find the truth for themselves. This may establish a communication contradiction which could leave the layman puzzled and confused. The structure denies the preacher's words. It basically leaves the truth and the answers in the hands of the clergy, and denies the ministry of the laity. Communication researchers speak of manifest and latent functions of communication. This may be one of the latent, or unintended functions of preaching as communication, and may be further defined as a *dysfunction,* or undesired effect.[11]

Another very important dysfunction may be the unintended buildup of hostility in a congregation owing to the absence of feedback. A significant piece of research was reported a few years ago on the role of feedback in the communication of information from a leader to his listeners. Harold J. Leavitt and Ronald Mueller set up an experiment in which a leader sought to describe a series of geometric patterns to a group of listeners so that the listeners would reproduce the patterns accurately. In one phase of the experiment, the instructor sat behind a partition and was not visible. This was termed "zero feedback." No questions or noises were permitted except by the instructor.

The second pattern was labeled the "visible audience" condition. The group members and instructor could see each other, but no speaking was allowed by the members. If they looked puzzled, the instructor was free to "read" this nonverbal communication and modify his message, but they could

[11] Charles R. Wright, "Functional Analysis and Mass Communication," in Lewis A. Dexter and David M. White, *People, Society and Mass Communications* (Glencoe: Free Press of Glencoe, 1964), p. 98.

not speak. The third pattern was one in which the instructor could ask questions to determine if he was being understood, but group members could only reply yes or no. The fourth pattern was a "free feedback" situation. In this case, the group members were allowed to interrupt the instructor, ask questions, and discuss the matter with each other.

The results of the Leavitt and Mueller studies revealed a steady increase of accuracy as feedback increased. With more feedback, the time required to complete the task also increased. However, an interesting by-product emerged. The researchers noticed that hostility built up in the group members when no feedback was permitted. The hostility was often vented on the leader of the session following the "no feedback" session.[12]

Now it should be noted that the sermon is a "zero feedback" situation. It is entirely possible that the absence of feedback on Sunday mornings results in the buildup of unconscious hostility in the members of the congregation, where they are allowed no opportunity to vent their feelings, doubts, or disagreements. Such hostility is, of course, considered inappropriate in the church. Therefore, it is possible that the tendency for church attenders to leave the front pews empty, seating themselves as far to the rear as possible, may be interpreted as a manifestation of this hostility. Poor attendance at worship may be another expression of this same feeling. It is possible that hostility on the part of those who attend regularly is not expressed as openly, but is manifested

12 Harold J. Leavitt and Ronald A. H. Mueller, "Some Effects of Feedback on Communication," *Human Relations*, IV (Spring, 1951), pp. 401–410.

by their indifference, their failure to really listen, and their low level of giving to the church. This whole area of the problem of hostility toward the minister, and hostility toward a communicator in general, deserves additional study and research. The Leavitt and Mueller studies seem to underscore the importance of building feedback or dialogue into the life of the churches.

Many other dimensions of communication theory and research are worthy of careful consideration by those who would proclaim the gospel, and little attention has yet been paid this rich mine of insights by the church and its leaders. The importance of a two-way flow of information, the new awareness that communication is incomplete unless it reaches the level of action, the importance of integrity between words and deeds, and the recognition that preaching as a medium is a message in itself are among the most crucial insights for an understanding of the preaching crisis.

Chapter V

PREACHING AS COMMUNICATION

It is now time to take a long, hard look at preaching. If preaching is a form of communication, and there is a body of scientific knowledge about the effectiveness of various types of communication, then it is high time to evaluate preaching from this perspective. We need to ask: How does preaching measure up as a tool for the communication of the gospel? What are its strengths and values? What are its weaknesses and its inadequacies?

Any realistic assessment of preaching must begin with the awareness that it is a form of mass communication. It is a form of transmitting messages to a large group of persons at once, and relies upon a one-way process with a minimum of feedback. Preaching as traditionally practiced is basically monologue, and there are some things we know about monological mass communication.

Research now indicates very strongly that mass communication functions best to reinforce the already existing attitudes of the audience. It may also be effective in influencing persons' opinions on matters in which they have no strong position one way or another. If the subject is new, or if the listener already leans toward the desired response, mass communication may be effective in influencing him. It may, for example, persuade him to try one brand of cigarettes rather than another if he already has some inclination toward the smoking of cigarettes.

However, if the result desired is to convert attitudes on controversial issues, or to influence behavior in a new direction not particularly desired by the listener, *mass communication usually has slight effect*. To quote one summary of important findings from communications research: "Mass communication can be effective in producing a shift on unfamiliar, lightly felt, peripheral issues—those that do not matter much to the audience or are not tied to audience predispositions. On the others, it is effective in reinforcing opinions but only infrequently changes them."[1]

THE MONOLOGICAL ILLUSION

It should be apparent that this research has very important implications for the pastor. If he relies on preaching to change the hearts of his people on racial integration, he may be wasting his time and building resistance. If he uses preaching almost exclusively to bear the burden of his communication task, he is surely putting too many of his begs in one asking.

[1] Bernard Berelson and G. A. Steiner, *Human Behavior: An Inventory of Scientific Findings* (New York: Harcourt, Brace & World, 1964), pp. 540–543.

If he uses preaching to reinforce the latent faith of his people in God and love for neighbor, he may expect some measure of success, assuming that they have a basis of faith to start with. To influence the congregation's deeply held racial attitudes, however, he will need to rely on methods that include dialogue.

The important point is that research increasingly points to the need for feedback or two-way communication in those instances when we hope to achieve comprehension of our message, acceptance, internalization, and action. To facilitate genuine communication, monologue is rarely enough and a two-way flow of information is almost essential. In our preaching efforts we have tended to rely heavily on one-way communication, assuming that this is sufficient to accomplish the goal of completely shared meaning. We have been satisfied simply to make contact with our listeners, *assuming* that nothing more is necessary in order to achieve complete communication. Some feedback cues are available to the preacher through facial expressions, gestures, or movements in the congregation, but he must be quite sensitive to catch them. The members of the congregation can "pass out in sleep or stalk out in anger, but they cannot talk back to the preacher," says Rolland W. Schloerb in his book on the preaching ministry.[2]

The absence of dialogue may be the key to understanding the failure of preaching to achieve the results in changed lives which we have always claimed for it. Occasionally, communication via the sermon occurs without feedback by the grace of God, but this seems to be the exception rather than the rule. Even then, we cannot be sure that the sermon event was not

[2] *Op. cit.,* p. 13.

surrounded by a context of dialogue and provided the climactic moment in a chain of circumstances!

Wayne E. Oates, a leading figure in the field of psychology and religion, has commented on the development of one-way communication in the life of the church in this very important quotation:

Historically, at least three things have happened to spiritual conversation between pastor and parishioner. First, the original proclamation of the Christian message was a two-way conversation in which Christians bore witness to what God had done in raising Christ from the dead. He had called them out of darkness into the light of the knowledge of God in the face of the living Christ. In return, those to whom they witnessed were free to converse with them, to inquire of them, and to discuss the meaning of the Scriptures in the light of those things. But, when the oratorical schools of the Western world laid hold of the Christian message, they made Christian preaching something vastly different. Oratory tended to take the place of conversation. The greatness of the orator took the place of the astounding event of Jesus Christ. And the dialogue between speaker and listener faded into a monologue.[3]

In his essay, "Experimental Preaching," Albert H. van den Heuvel supports the historical accuracy of Oates's analysis. He points out that through the centuries preaching has become more and more the task of the priest or theologian, and speaks of the traditional Reformed service as a one-man show. "With the great exceptions of Methodism and the Pentecostal tradition, in which the man spoke who was moved to speak, because he had something to contribute to all, the old tradition has been replaced by the sweating full-timer who, Sabbath after Sabbath, prepares his one or two sermons."[4]

[3] *Protestant Pastoral Counseling* (Philadelphia: Westminster Press, 1962), p. 167.
[4] *The Humiliation of the Church* (Philadelphia: Westminster Press, 1966), p. 70.

If it is indeed true that the early Christian groups placed more emphasis on dialogue, this may help to explain their tremendous vitality. It may also explain why that creative life is often missing in Christian fellowships, and help us understand the dynamic quality of Pentecostal groups where dialogue and mutual witnessing is stressed.

In *The Miracle of Dialogue*, Reuel L. Howe has pointed out how many of us naïvely believe that communication takes place simply by telling people "what they ought to know." He speaks of this as the "monological illusion," and comments out of his experience with the Institute for Advanced Pastoral Studies that "young ministers are disillusioned about the effectiveness of preaching and suspect that 'telling' is not a sure means of communication, but because they know of no alternative they are caught in the one-way street of monologue."[5]

Small Groups Provide Dialogue

The absence of dialogue in the preaching situation may also help to explain the low level of involvement of the average church member, and the surprising lack of basic Christian commitment on the part of those who have attended church for years.

If the goal of preaching is action, and if feedback is essential to the achievement of deeper levels of communication, we may assume that when dialogue is built in, the minister's efforts to communicate the gospel will be enhanced. It seems a reasonable hypothesis that the many small study

[5] New York: The Seabury Press, 1963, p. 32.

and discussion groups which have appeared in church life in recent years would provide a feedback effect. In this case, even though the sermon itself may not be talked about in the group, the discussion of the content of the Christian faith establishes an indirect dialogue with the minister's preaching. Members of such groups may be expected to reveal a deeper involvement in the preached message and in the life of the church as a result of their group experience.

That this hypothesis indeed has validity was indicated by a research project I conducted to explore this possibility. Several clues stimulated this effort. The book, *Spiritual Renewal through Personal Groups,* edited by John L. Casteel, contains reports from a number of writers on small group ventures in church life. Thomas M. Steen wrote that as a result of his experiences with small groups "a new depth and vitality" had been born in his preaching. He reported further that he found "more of true listening to the sermon because I am preaching with them and not for or at them."[6] A member of another church reported in the same volume that as a result of his group experience, "Now I find in worship and preaching what has been there all the time, but which now speaks to *me.*"[7]

Dr. Casteel supported this link between preaching and small groups when he wrote: "I am quite sure that there is a deep relation between preaching and such means of life in the church as the small groups represent. Everywhere one encounters these groups one discovers that there is an influence exerted by them on the preaching that goes on in the church."[8]

[6] New York: Association Press, 1957, p. 44.
[7] *Ibid.,* p. 119.
[8] Letter from Casteel, October 27, 1959.

The effects of belonging to a small personal group, and the relationship between group membership and preaching in particular, were then explored.

I visited twelve small groups as a participant-observer, including Bible study groups and sermon discussion groups. I collected information from 105 members of the twelve groups, and from ten ministers of the churches in which the groups were located. I wanted to know if participation in a small group influenced the individual's ability to understand the sermon and maintain interest and attention during the preaching.

The results indicated a strong, positive relationship between group participation and responsiveness to preaching. Nearly three-fourths of the group members reported an increase in their ability to understand the sermon. A majority reported that their minister's sermons spoke to their condition more after they joined a group, and nearly 75 per cent indicated that their interest and attention during the preaching of the sermon had increased since joining a group. In addition, there was a noticeable increase in their attendance at worship and in their leadership activity in the church after joining a group.[9] A few sample comments by group members follow:

This group provides an anvil on which to pound out what one believes; I believe that my own faith has been strengthened, or established, by what we do in the group. . . .

I think I have learned more in one year than in all the years of church attendance.

[9] For a more detailed report on this research, see my article, "Preaching and the Nature of Communication," in *Pastoral Psychology*, October, 1963, or my Th.D. dissertation, "Two-way Communication through Small Groups in Relation to Preaching," Boston University, 1960.

I feel that belonging to this group, acquiring the attitudes and feeling the closeness of God contributes greatly to my ability to worship at the church service on Sunday. My attention wanders less and I am more "at one" with God during the service.

One of the significant differences revealed by this data was related to length of time in a group. Those who had been members of a group for a longer period of time indicated more change than those with shorter membership. This may help to explain why some of the efforts to promote small groups meet with disappointing results; the planners may be looking for results too soon, before a significant level of trust and relationship has developed.

The ministers also reported values in their small group programs. Nine of the ten interviewed testified that their sermon preparation had been influenced by the feedback gained through the groups. They found stimulation and guidance for their sermons and came to know their people and their needs better. Most also reported that parishioners involved in small groups increased in attentiveness and sensitivity to their preaching. The ministers' reports verified the information from the group members themselves, indicating an increase in understanding of the sermon as well as an increase in attendance and leadership activity.

The Rev. Otis E. Young was recently asked the following question: "What relationship do you see, if any, between the small group program in your church and preaching?" His reply underscores the thesis that participation in a small group supports the preaching ministry:

There is certainly a direct relationship between these small groups, particularly ours which meet weekly, and preaching. I find that it helps my preaching. Through these regular intensive contacts, I am constantly made more aware of what's really bothering people. Many of my sermons have grown out of these groups. Often in our meetings we talk about the sermon and I get comments on what was understood and what was not understood. All of the persons in these groups have said that their experience in them has made the sermon much more relevant and meaningful. In fact they testify that the whole worship service has taken on more meaning. I am convinced that groups such as these are almost an imperative for relevant preaching in our time.[10]

In summary, this research demonstrated that participation in a small group, where dialogue on the meanings of the gospel takes place, results in a deeper interest and involvement in preaching. These findings are consistent with communication research, which increasingly emphasizes the importance of feedback and a two-way flow if communication is to move beyond contact to action.

PREACHING AS OVERCOMMUNICATION

The parable of the complacent sower, in which the farmer sows his seed over and over with no concern for preparing the ground or cultivating the crop, is meant to portray the problem of overcommunication. One of the great dilemmas in the present pattern of church life is the sheer volume of information we present to our congregations. Week after week, we present them with additional ideas, concepts, duties, and responsibilities, with no opportunity to talk back, to wrestle with those ideas, to absorb and integrate the content before we dump some more. It is little wonder the seed lies on top of

10 Personal correspondence. For a fuller statement of the group program in his ministry, see Young's article, "A Reorientation to All of Life," *Pastoral Psychology*, March, 1967.

the ground and does not put down roots in the lives of the listeners. We so saturate our people with a barrage of words and ideas that they become frustrated with their lack of opportunity to raise questions, express reactions, and compare understandings. They simply do not hear any longer. In a deep psychological sense, then, we have an empty pulpit today, for its words are not heard by the man in the pew.

I once described this pattern to Dr. David Manning White, graduate professor of journalism in Boston University's School of Public Communication and a leading figure in modern communication research. Dr. White's immediate reaction was to say, "This is a classic case of overcommunication." We are presenting more content than our people can absorb. Or to put it another way, we do not supplement the sermon with adequate structures which could allow them the opportunity to wrestle with that content and appropriate it as their own. As a result, much of our communication effort is surely wasted. Elton Trueblood put it this way: "People are sermon-hardened; they've heard too much."

There is another dimension to the problem of overcommunication, and that is the relation between speaking and silence. We Protestants understand very little about the role and importance of silence in religious communication. The Quakers and others who have explored the realm of silence have much to teach us. For example, we need to learn how to creatively alternate words with silence in order for the words to take on significance and depth.

The preachers I hear today seem to be anxiously filling the silence with words. It doesn't seem to matter much what the words are—just so they are words. The ideas don't seem to

build on one another; it is as though the preacher is filling the
silence by free association, rather than a disciplined turning of
one great thought. He is building words on other words, with
no breathing space between them. The thought of Max
Picard, a Swiss writer, is directly relevant to this problem:

> When language is no longer related to silence, it loses its source of
> refreshment and renewal and therefore something of its substance.
> Language today seems to talk automatically, out of its own strength,
> and, emptying and scattering itself, it seems to be hastening to an
> end. There is something hard and obstinate in language today, as
> though it were making a great effort to remain alive in spite of its
> emptiness. . . . By taking it away from silence we have made lan-
> guage an orphan.[11]

Furthermore, as part of our clergy-dependence pattern, we
ask our preachers to speak so much that they have nothing
creative and original left to say. The preacher is emptying his
well of creativity faster than it can be replenished. The result
is that he has gone dry. The pumps go on drawing a thin
stream of silt from the bottom of the well, but it is not very
refreshing to the thirsty seeker who awaits the living water.
The minister who would preach to others must alternate his
own speaking with the experience of creative silence so his
words will have meaning. Too often, the only refreshment the
preacher finds consists of listening to more words by other
preachers.

The overcommunication problem is often manifested in the
fact that ministers tend to preach too long. They blunt the
message they offer by going on and on, while their weary
listeners shift in their seats, look at their watches, and ponder

[11] The World of Silence, trans. Stanley Godman (Chicago: Henry
Regnery Company, 1952), p. 41.

the social consequences of leaving before the closing hymn. We preachers speak too long precisely because we have nothing to say. We keep on in the hope that something will emerge from our many words, and also because it is comforting to be in the center of attention. I recently heard a distinguished layman remind a group of ministers that they have a heavy ego involvement in keeping the preaching structure as it is. The minister's enjoyment of his preaching privilege is a major barrier to the development of new forms of communication.

We live in a time when we are bombarded and surrounded with words, ideas, and messages from all sides. In an earlier time, when there were fewer messages and more silence, preaching was more likely to be heard. Now we speak too much and say too little. It seems obvious that we need to provide pools of silence in our worship, in order that the presence of God may be experienced and the words of the faith may be heard. The time is ripe for us to learn the lesson of silence to counteract our overcommunication.

The Problem of Paid Witness

Even where preaching has become part of a context of dialogue, there are problems inherent in the very structure which sets apart one full-time paid member of the congregation as *the one* to do the proclaiming of the gospel. In the first place, the very fact that a clergyman is paid to proclaim his Christian witness blunts that witness immeasurably. It has nowhere been noted more cogently than in the words of Martin, a character in C. P. Snow's novel, *The Affair:*

Oh yes, Julian . . . we know that you believe that. It's like G. H. Hardy's old crack—If the Archbishop of Canterbury says he believes in God, that's all in the way of business, but if he says he doesn't, one can take it he means what he says. . . .[12]

This comment, couched in an offhand remark of a character in a novel, is really a penetrating criticism of the professionalism of the Church's witness and should not be shrugged off lightly. How can we take a man's words with utter seriousness when we know his salary is dependent upon his saying those words whether he believes them or not?

When one person is set aside and delegated to perform the bulk of the church's work, this actually prevents the rest of the congregation from having a vital share in that effort. By centering the ministerial functions in one person, we suppress the role of the laity or reduce it to running errands for the "real" minister. The result is an inability on the part of the laity to perform or even comprehend their legitimate ministry.

Arnold Come has reminded us in his courageous book, *Agents of Reconciliation,* that in the New Testament concept of the church's ministry all members of the church were God's servants or ministers.[13] In the early church there was no distinction of status between those who had the gift of preaching or teaching or healing. The man with a gift for preaching was not regarded as a more "holy" Christian than the others, a concept that plagues the church today. Every member was empowered with a unique gift of ministry and was expected to exercise that gift. And all gifts were regarded as of equal importance.

[12] New York: Charles Scribner's Sons, 1960, p. 75.
[13] Philadelphia: Westminster Press, 1960, p. 80.

This shared ministry is virtually lost today, although the current emphasis on the ministry of the laity is an attempt to revive it. We have centered all our ministry in our paid professionals and thereby sold our birthright for a padded pew, a comfortable arrangement for both the elevated, hyperactive preacher and the silent, inert layman. So long as this structure goes unchallenged, so long is the layman dependent upon the professional minister to do his witnessing, his studying, and his praying for him. Dependence is appropriate in childhood, but the longer it is prolonged the more it stifles growth and prevents movement toward the "mature manhood" of which Paul writes in Ephesians 4:13.

There is another pernicious problem involved when one man is expected to speak his authentic Christian witness every Sunday or even several times a week. If one must produce a message whether he has anything to say or not, his preaching often becomes artificial, formalized, and wooden, lacking in power and authenticity. His sermon illustrations tend to be drawn from books of illustrations if he uses them at all. How can his message be fresh and authentic when he has not been able to have enough fresh experience of life to feed his preaching? The normal parish duties of the average minister do not allow him to drink that deeply of life's experiences. As a result, he is dependent upon the religious experiences of others which he finds in books and attempts to quote or paraphrase to his audience. His listeners are well aware of the difference when he speaks from the depths of his own religious experience and when he is parroting the experience and insight of someone else. They sense the absence of reality in what he is saying and the false ring in his affirmations.

To be sure, there are ministers who have learned how to relate deeply to life and whose sermons reflect that fact. They are men who have discovered how to be sensitive to the feedback offered them and how to be open to depth experiences through their pastoral visits and counseling. Men who have developed such sensitivity are all too few.

By expecting every minister to have the gift of preaching, and by expecting him to exercise that gift on a time schedule, we may blunt the genuine gifts he has to offer, and force him to produce a gift for which he may have no great talent. Then we wonder why he does not inspire us week after week!

WHY NO CHANGE?

If so many factors point to the shortcomings of our present pattern of reliance on preaching, why does it persist? If preaching is really one-way communication which does not change behavior to any great extent, why is it so enduring? If preaching tends to become superficial, artificial, and rarely beneficial, why is it so staunchly defended as God's appointed way?

For one thing, preaching makes for a predictable situation. Since nothing earth-shaking is likely to result from a sermon, one can count on the relative safety of going to church. Further, preaching makes for a comfortable relationship with God. If the message is a little too threatening, it can easily be ignored or forgotten. The preaching situation flatters the minister's ego and leaves the layman free to continue living as before. There is very little threat to the status quo in preaching, and very little threat to the individual and his way of doing things.

We may say that preaching supports the unconscious conspiracy between clergy and laity to keep things comfortable and safe, yet provide a little "religious" inspiration. In my earlier book, *The God-Evaders*, I have written at length about this "law of religious evasion," in which we structure our church life so as to keep God out—or at arm's length.[14] The preaching structure is one of the ways in which we give God an inch but keep a yard for ourselves, unmolested by the cutting edge of the gospel.

There is another element about which we know very little, but which I have sensed very strongly at times. Preaching often seems to provide an emotional outlet for the minister's personal problems. One can often hear the minister's despair or sense of futility pouring out through his sermon, quite apart from the content of his subject. This personal catharsis can be heard in his choice of words and symbols at times, but also in the feelings he projects. When those feelings are inappropriate to the subject material, it seems more apparent that he is communicating at several levels at once. When this process of preaching as personal therapy for the minister gets in the way of creative communication of the gospel, it is time to ask if the preaching structure is adequate to the demands placed upon it. It may also help explain why the minister is hesitant to give it up.

Furthermore, the introduction of dialogue is threatening to both clergy and laity. It means that the minister is exposed to the possibility of embarrassing questions he may not be able to answer. He may lose his position on the pedestal. It may mean some dominant individual may talk too much if given the chance to talk at all. It may mean that one may be called to

14 New York: Harper & Row, 1966.

account for what he says. It is much easier and safer to go on spinning out the monologue than to open Pandora's box by introducing the threat of return communication.

The Covered Ears Theory

Here is a theory which may help us to understand the puzzling problem of the sermon and the role it plays in our culture. It may be that the primary reason we listen to sermons is not to hear the objective content of the message at all. It may be that there is a deeper psychological satisfaction provided by the very process of sitting through the sermon no matter what is said from the pulpit. I feel this is a distinct possibility, and I find one clue in the way my children sometimes listen when I insist on "sounding off" to them.

At times when my son has been misbehaving, I choose that moment to lecture to him briefly on life in general—a common parental failing. He may stand dutifully looking me in the eye as though listening, but the nonverbal communication tells me he is not. He is really saying, "Okay, I've got it coming. Go ahead and get it over with. I know I have to go through this." When younger, he even covered his ears while I talked if he was feeling especially rebellious. He would stand there until I had finished, but *his ears were covered*. Children are very clever at letting us indulge ourselves while appearing to listen, but they can use the time well for planning their next act of independence.

I wonder if many people do not come to the sermon *with their ears covered*. On an unconscious level, they come to fulfill a deep inner longing to be lectured at, without particularly caring about the content of the message. They come to satisfy this more subjective or emotional need—the need to be lectured at or "dressed down." As a result the sermon seems "relevant" to their need to be talked at by "Father," so they do not notice the irrelevance of the message. Other persons in the congregation may be listening more deeply for the content of the sermon, and may become upset when it seems weak.

If this covered ears theory of preaching has validity, it would help to explain why many people continue to attend church even when they are not listening to the minister's message. They may be experiencing an unconscious sense of being punished and having atoned for their misdeeds simply by going through the motions of sitting quietly and appearing to listen. As a result, they go away feeling whole and clean or forgiven. The minister, for his part, could go away feeling satisfied that he has "straightened his children out," which makes him feel important and fulfilled.[15] The covered ears theory may also help us understand why only one person in five can tell us the main idea in the minister's sermon following the service.

The difficulty with this exchange is that it is a father-child transaction. It leaves the father feeling satisfied, but it also leaves the parishioner a "child" in the faith. The very structure of the sermon is a dependence structure in which the "children" sit at the father's feet while he does all the talking. Regrettably, they do not mature in the process, but are expected to return next week for a repeat experience. In a

[15] See the recent book by William Stephenson, *The Play Theory of Mass Communication* (Chicago: University of Chicago Press, 1967), for some suggestive thinking on the subjective meanings of communication.

time when man is slowly learning to grow up and is seeking structures which allow him to express himself as an *adult,* the father-child structures like preaching will hold less and less satisfaction for him.

The covered ears theory does not pretend to be the whole answer, but it may be worth further research as one important dimension in the preaching crisis.

WHAT FUTURE FOR PREACHING?

While I have brought together a summary of criticisms of the preaching structure, I do not want to be misunderstood. I am not suggesting that preaching has no value. I am not proposing that we eliminate all preaching (which would be a futile proposal anyway). What I do believe is that we misuse and overuse preaching.

It is the reliance upon *preaching alone* to bear the burden of our communication task which is erroneous. It is our expectation that preaching will automatically result in action in terms of Christian living on Monday through Saturday which is naïve. It is our emphasis upon preaching and the resulting devaluation of the witness of the laity which is bad strategy.

Preaching does have a legitimate and important role. Preaching can properly and appropriately be used: (1) to inspire by the proclamation of God's good news; (2) to bring new and relevant information to the gathered people of a congregation; (3) to challenge with a new vision; (4) to reinforce present attitudes; (5) to comfort and strengthen in times of crisis; and (6) for other purposes. However, preaching need not and, indeed, should not be the whole task of one man.

It is important that Christian groups have the opportunity to hear the personal and spoken witness of those who have experienced the realities of their faith or who have unusual insight. These persons may be clergy or laity, men or women, youth or the elderly. If we did not have to endure so much mediocre preaching, the occasional sermon with a clear purpose by someone with an important message would have much greater impact. I am not against preaching. I hunger for the great sermon. I am opposed to dull, wooden preaching Sunday after Sunday by those who have little gift for it and no enthusiasm.

It is the every-Sunday structure in which we have encased preaching that must be changed. We preach too much, so that it has virtually no effect. We should preach less, and do a better job when we do. This calls for more responsible and inspired preaching growing out of genuine experience which cries out to be shared. But perhaps we should stop expecting every minister to be the gifted preacher he can't be anyway. As Hendrik Kraemer has put it, in *The Communication of the Christian Faith,* we have "idolized" preaching and developed a "great inhibition toward all other means of communication. . . ."[16] He also wrote that our "extravagant and nearly exclusive stress on verbal communication, on preaching and sermonizing" is a "degeneration or distortion" of Reformation teaching.[17]

In the concluding chapter, I will propose some alternative

[16] Philadelphia: Westminster Press, 1956, p. 75.
[17] *Ibid.,* p. 27.

structures which take into account the need for a change in our present reliance upon preaching.

Summary

The concept of communication as a dynamic two-way process has important implications for a new theory of preaching. Preaching as ordinarily understood is one-way communication in which the preacher receives a minimum of feedback. His listeners cannot question him, raise doubts, or express themselves; their role is a passive role. Preaching, as communication, is an incomplete process unless it is supplemented with dialogue.

One of the aims of Christian communication is the meeting of mind with mind, the encounter of heart with heart and self with self—a dialogical relationship. Preaching rarely, if ever, achieves this end. One man is set apart, placed in an exalted position in the pulpit, and expected to establish a dialogical relationship with a mass of people. Our understanding of the nature of communication now helps us realize how futile this effort is when preaching is relied upon as the major communication tool.

Preaching as an isolated event in itself is an inadequate vehicle for the communication of the gospel. That preaching has an important place in the life of the church cannot be denied. It should be seen, however, not as an isolated event, but as one link in a communications chain which includes personal contacts, small group relationships, shared experiences, common study, audio-visual exposure, and joint action in serving the world.

Chapter VI

BEYOND PREACHING

I t should now be apparent that the problem of preaching is rooted in the nature of communication. As research has revealed crucial insights into the communication process, so should we begin to modify our structures in the churches to conform to these new insights and improve our ability to share the good news of God. What should be the direction for the future? What new shape or pattern will emerge for the church of tomorrow?

The first and most important statement we in the churches must be willing to make is that we do not know the full answer. We cannot say with any certainty what the shape and pattern of the communication of the gospel should be for the church of tomorrow. God has not yet clearly revealed it to us. Or perhaps, we should say that we have not yet been sufficiently willing to give up our obsession with the past and seek his will in the matter. We are a pilgrim people, and as in the past we are called to set out on a new exodus with no sure knowledge of our destination—a pilgrimage of faith.

In a recently published book on preaching and the renewal of the church, the author joins the ranks of those who charge from the lists on a great white steed to defend preaching:

> The current disposition to denigrate preaching—the formal act of heralding the good news to one hundred or one thousand people in a sanctuary—weakens the church's God-given ministry. Forthright biblical preaching which avoids the marginal (shallow moralism) and penetrates to the heart of man's profound dilemma (guilt and meaninglessness) and speaks to his loneliness persuades persons to repent, encourages them to trust God, and gives them identity. Linked with evangelical teaching, it motivates and equips them to exercise Christ's ministry in the world.[1]

To denigrate means to blacken or defame. I haven't found many people trying to blacken or defame preaching. And that is certainly not *my* intent. As I understand them, the present-day critics of preaching are trying to be honest about the seriousness of the problem which is represented in our preaching crisis today. It certainly does not help us to take an honest look at the problem if we dismiss the critics of preaching as the devil's advocates. Rather than weakening the church's ministry, it may strengthen us to challenge our outmoded structures.

A YESTERDAY-STRUCTURE

The net effect of the current defenses of preaching is to say that yesterday's structures are good enough for today and even

[1] Wallace Fisher, *Preaching and Parish Renewal* (Nashville: Abingdon Press, 1966), p. 17.

tomorrow. If this is so, it means that the church is the only realm of life in which this holds true. For change is the keynote of our age, and it would indeed be remarkable if our lives should be affected at every point save one. It is now time to recognize that the old preaching pattern is a yesterday-structure. This is the pattern of relying upon preaching to bear the *major burden* of God's communication with his people, with no dialogue structures to permit discussion of the *content* of the gospel message and to reflect on common action.

It is this old preaching structure, which elevates the clergy-man to a position of special status over the passive laity, which is a yesterday-structure. This preaching pattern, which relies upon the brilliance of the minister's speaking ability to hold the church together, belongs to the past. We must now call into question the preaching pattern which limits the layman's response to a greeting at the church door. The results are not consistent with the message we proclaim.

If there is one thing needed in our churches today, it is a commitment to flexibility of styles, the honesty to admit that yesterday's patterns may not be good enough anymore, an openness to experiment with new structures of church life, the courage to risk failure in order to discover new truth. Anyone who tells us that "what was good enough for grandma is good enough for us" simply does not understand the seriousness of the situation. We now need churches which are structured toward the future, with no sacred cows such as the idolization of the sermon to block their life and impede the movement of the spirit. *Nothing in our present church structures is sacred, irrevocable, given by God for all time, preach-*

ing included. There is nothing we are now doing that we may not be able to do more effectively another way.

It seems clear that we are in an interim period in regard to our church structures. We now know that the old yesterday-structures are not enough. We do not yet see clearly what the tomorrow-structures may be, though some signs are present in our midst. What we can affirm is that there are some possible *today*-structures—tentative steps toward the future. I will indicate what some of these today-structures are, with the realization that even to change at all from yesterday calls for flexibility and a commitment to openness.

Today-Structures: Building in Dialogue

We need to be realistic. Preaching will be with us for some time. As an institution, it is deeply established within our traditions. If we now understand that preaching alone is inadequate, and if we also know that genuine communication is enhanced by a two-way flow of information, the next step should be plain. It is our clear and present responsibility to build dialogue structures into the life of our churches. As Reuel Howe has said, "The Church's preaching is not a one-way communication from the preacher to the congregation, but a two-way dialogical relationship."[2] A number of dialogue models have been and are being used today.

Model A—Preaching Plus Discussion. In this model, opportunity to discuss the sermon is provided sometime during the week that follows. At times, ministers have paused

[2] "The Recovery of Dialogue in Preaching," *Pastoral Psychology,* October, 1961, p. 10.

after their sermon, and opened the floor for questions and response before continuing the worship service. While this has some advantage, it permits only a few to speak out and comes as a radical break with past tradition. It also contains the clear danger that one or two "cranks" may take over the floor, and they can be very difficult to head off. This approach has minimal value for the majority of those present.

I have heard of one church in which the entire congregation divides into small groups for discussion immediately after the sermon, returning to the sanctuary to complete the worship service after the discussion period. The obvious advantage of this style is that it involves every member of the congregation. Other ministers have arranged for those who wish to remain after the service to meet in another room to discuss the sermon. In one church where I observed this pattern, the minister absented himself for most of the discussion period to allow more freedom for the expression of disagreements and negative feelings. A lay moderator led the discussion. The minister then appeared for a while to clarify particular questions which may have arisen. Again, the disadvantage is that only a small percentage of the congregation is involved in the dialogue.

The Rev. Howard L. Abbott has reported an experiment in the Northfield Congregational Church (United Church of Christ) in Northfield, Connecticut. Abbott found that so many church families were away on summer weekends that Sunday attendance dropped sharply. As an experiment, the Sunday services were abandoned in July and August and a Wednesday evening service instituted. A new format was introduced in which a twenty- to thirty-minute service with a

brief sermon was held in the sanctuary, but before the benediction was pronounced the group moved downstairs for coffee
and discussion of the sermon. Worship and discussion are
understood as a unity, and the benediction is not pronounced
until the close of the discussion period. At times, the group
has divided into smaller discussion groups, and at other times,
remained together as one large discussion group.

The First Reformed Church in Schenectady, New York,
also has an interesting dialogue format. Morning worship
begins at ten o'clock each Sunday, followed by an hour during
which three options are open to the worshiper who remains.
He may attend a large discussion meeting on some social or
personal problem related to Christian commitment and every-
day life. These sessions are planned by a committee of laymen. He may elect instead a Bible study section. If he is a
youth, he may attend a youth discussion group on theology
and the theater. The church also offers a Wednesday noon
"dialogue luncheon." While others eat, the leader for the day
makes a fifteen-minute presentation, followed by a thirty-
minute period of discussion.[3]

It is openness to try new methods which will help our
churches discover more vital communication patterns, and
sermon discussion models can be helpful.

Model B—The Sermon Seminar. In his book, *Parish Back
Talk,* Browne Barr describes a pattern which is being used in
a number of churches. In this sermon seminar approach
(which may be called the "serminar"), a group of parishioners
meet with the minister one night a week to wrestle with the
text and the issues of the sermon. In Barr's church, the

[3] Personal correspondence from the Rev. J. Dean Dykstra.

minister scheduled to preach the following Sunday presents a brief background for the scripture of the week, in order to make clear the basic meaning of the passage.

Then the seminar divides into small groups of eight or ten persons to discuss the passage for forty minutes. The preacher sits with one of the groups, primarily as listener. The groups then reassemble for brief reports. As Barr puts it, "in the process witnessing and confession and doubting and support have taken place. Sometimes Christian discipline and rebuke have been experienced profitably. . . ."[4] The evening closes with a fifteen-minute period of prayer, and on occasion members of the group offer brief spoken prayers. During Lent, the pattern is modified to include a larger segment of the congregation gathered in neighborhood groups, with the minister's introduction via radio. Other variations of the sermon seminar in Barr's congregation have included breakfast meetings, downtown luncheon meetings, and meetings in members' homes.

The sermon seminars have helped the preacher to become aware of the realistic pressures and problems of his people as he preaches, but it helps them, too. A more recent report on this program in Barr's church indicates that participants gain in their understanding of the Bible, their sense of belonging to a fellowship, and in their appreciation of prayer. They come to Sunday service "invariably eager to hear the sermon," for they are more deeply involved in it.[5]

The sermon seminar idea found an early expression in the

[4] *Parish Back Talk, op. cit.,* pp. 76–82.
[5] Mary M. Eakin, "Sermon Seminar in a Parish Church," *The Christian Century,* January 19, 1966.

postwar work of Horst Symanowski in Germany. A leader in the German Evangelical Academy movement, Symanowski has written of his experiments with small groups of workers gathered weekly to review his sermon with him. Meeting on Friday evenings, the group would listen to a summary of the main ideas of the sermon to be preached the following Sunday. While many of these men would never darken the door of the church, their responses to the sermon were helpful to the preacher by providing a reality-testing function. Ministers in this country have been influenced by Symanowski to experiment with this pattern.[6]

Model C—Ongoing Small Groups. In the past decade in America, there has been a small group explosion in the life of the Protestant churches. This development has been documented in such books as John L. Casteel's *Spiritual Renewal Through Personal Groups,* soon to be issued in a new version. This development still appears to be very strong. Study groups, discussion groups, and prayer groups have appeared in large numbers, even where the minister was not supportive of the groups. They seem to have answered the real hunger of some for a deeper spiritual life than the average Sunday service offers them. As already described in an earlier chapter, research into these groups indicates that they provide a two-way flow of communication that strengthens the minister's preaching efforts. They continue to be one alternative for building dialogue into the life of the church, and have the advantage of providing ongoing fellowships in which some measure of sharing one another's burdens and mutual ministry may develop.

[6] Symanowski, *The Christian Witness in an Industrial Society,* trans. George H. Kehm (Philadelphia: Westminster Press, 1964), pp. 90–91.

Model D—The East Harlem Model. In *The Congregation in Mission,* George W. Webber has described an interesting variation on the small group approach. In the East Harlem Protestant Parish, members meet weekly in small neighborhood Bible study groups. The sermon text for the following Sunday is also the passage to be studied in the neighborhood groups. Staff members meet later in the week and share insights from these discussions with the scheduled preacher. When he speaks that Sunday, he has the advantage of those members of the congregation having been involved in a study of the passage and in having fed the sermon to some extent. This method has much to commend it. Says Webber:

> In the inner city, where the Bible is being taken seriously, preaching is biblical through and through. The preacher defines his task as "breaking open" the word of God to the congregation. For preaching to have integrity, however, the congregation is required to be as fully involved as the preacher. The proclamation of the word depends not only upon the faithfulness of the minister, but also upon the corporate involvement of the whole people of God. When the members of a congregation are engaged in a continuing study of the Bible they also are able to enter into the preaching of the word as active participants in a dialogue. Preaching is a corporate act and demands participation.[7]

Model E—Church of the Saviour Model. The remarkable Church of the Saviour in Washington, D.C. maintains a number of mission groups, which consist of a core of committed church members plus other interested and concerned persons drawn to a particular mission task. Most of the mission groups meet weekly for worship, study, and time for personal sharing. The accomplishments of some of these groups has been amazing, and Elizabeth O'Connor's book,

[7] Nashville: Abingdon Press, 1964, p. 82.

Call to Commitment, is the story of this church and its patterns of life.[8] Here again, the dialogue on the content of the gospel is established in small groups, but the element of being called to a particular task is an added dimension.

An interesting development has emerged recently in the Potter's House, the unique coffee house of the Church of the Saviour. A Sunday worship service is now being tried on an experimental basis, with worshipers seated around the tables where they usually sip espresso and eat sandwiches. Tape-recorded music replaces the organ and choir. Laymen serve as leaders for the service, reading a simple litany and giving a short spoken meditation. This is followed by fifteen minutes of silence, then music is again played as coffee and rolls are served. A period of questions and discussion allows participants an opportunity to express themselves before the closing portion of the litany is read and the benediction pronounced. Interest in this venture has been very high, and persons are often turned away because the seats are filled. A forthcoming book by Elizabeth O'Connor will describe this experiment in more detail, and it will be watched with great interest as a possible style that might be used widely.[9]

Model F—Sermon-replacement Models. A recent five-column headline in *The New York Times* read as follows: "Film of Negro Child's Life Replaces Sermon at Judson Memorial." At Judson Memorial Church in New York City, a new film by church member Robert Newman was shown in place of the sermon. Discussion followed. Apparently interest

[8] New York: Harper & Row, 1963, ch. 10.
[9] Elizabeth O'Connor, "The Coffee House Church," *Harvest,* April, 1966. Newsletter of the Church of the Saviour, Washington, D.C.

was high. The minister, the Rev. Howard Moody, said: "The visual can sometimes be more powerful than the spoken. We decided to see if a film could do a better job than a spoken sermon."[10]

There is considerable evidence that dramatic new forms are beginning to replace the traditional sermon. A national magazine reports that many ministers are substituting movies, plays, or poetry readings for conventional sermons. Parishioners at St. Clement's Episcopal Church in Manhattan have presented a portion of Harold Pinter's play *The Caretaker* and other dramatic readings in place of the sermon. The chaplain at a Southern university has projected pictures from a magazine onto the chapel wall in order to illustrate his point.

In *The Comfortable Pew*, Pierre Berton asks why it is that churches cannot consider some of the new techniques of communications as alternatives to the sermon. Says Berton:

> It is not in the cards that every ordained man should be or indeed need be a powerful speaker or pulpit personality. Yet there are in the Church some men whose value lies in their ability to stir souls, rekindle emotions, and communicate eternal truths in a fresh, relevant, and compelling manner. Why should such men be confined to a single church or a single congregation? If doctors, advertising men, business tycoons, and even schools can use closed-circuit television to reach hundreds of thousands of people who would not otherwise receive the message, why should the Church not be using it too, to bring its most inspired spokesmen to the attention of larger numbers of churchgoers?[11]

Particularly when the opportunity to discuss the message is included, this kind of imaginative programming can relieve

---

[10] *New York Times*, October 17, 1966.
[11] *The Comfortable Pew, op. cit.*, pp. 101–102.

the monotony of constant preaching and possibly counteract some of the disadvantages of the preaching structure.

Model G—The Retreat Model. Another alternative method of building in dialogue is to conduct a weekend retreat occasionally for a segment of the church membership. In this way, there would not be ongoing dialogue, but there would be opportunity for a core group to have an experience of dialogue in depth on the meanings of their faith. I do not refer here to church planning conferences, where the main business is planning church programs. I refer rather to a spiritual retreat, including worship and discussion on a theme with significant religious content. The retreat model is often used to supplement one of the other models mentioned already.

Whatever models are adopted for including dialogue in the life of the church, there are some basic criteria for evaluating such efforts. First, the content of the Christian faith—beliefs, values, doubts—should be discussed freely, and practical applications of the faith considered. Too many of our church groups and meetings discuss money, program action, but *not* faith, so they have no opportunity for these basic considerations.

A second point which should be observed when possible is that the same people should be held together in groups of fifteen or less over a period of time. A mutual ministry can then emerge in their midst and there is opportunity for them to become a primary group. In this way, Christian concepts like love of neighbor and forgiveness can be experienced as present realities, not just distant concepts.

The third feature I consider desirable is that the dialogue

structure should be one in which personal content—feelings and concerns—can be shared, and trust can emerge.

A fourth criterion deals with the leadership pattern. If the discussion remains centered in the minister, then we are maintaining a dependence pattern. Ideally, the minister's task is to free the dialogue *among his people* so that he becomes simply a catalyst and becomes unnecessary himself. This way he is free to move on and stimulate dialogue elsewhere. When all discussion is centered in the minister, then he can only relate to a small number of persons on a one-to-one basis, and is soon exhausted.

It should be apparent that we can build dialogue structures which are merely superficial and do not touch people's lives very deeply. We can in this way generate a little deeper interest on the part of some, without basically threatening them by a radical confrontation of the gospel. The Christian faith is a costly faith, and a lukewarm Christian is no Christian.

This also points to another very important truth—that communication and community are closely related. Communication flourishes where there is a sense of genuine community, an aura of trust and acceptance. Community appears where communication is genuine and honest. *Without significant two-way communication, we cannot expect a deep sense of community to appear in our churches.* This helps us to understand why our churches often reveal very superficial levels of community; there has been no significant communication among the members, so no community could emerge. Do we want Christian community badly enough to pay the price of costly, even painful communication with each other?

BEYOND PREACHING: TOMORROW-STRUCTURES

We are not entirely without suggestions for the future shape of the church's communication of the gospel. Some have proposed that we declare a moratorium on all pulpit preaching for a year or longer. While we haven't found many takers for this suggestion as yet, it might be an exciting experiment for a risk-taking church to try. The goal would be to see if more imaginative and effective methods of communicating the gospel could be developed. Some intense dialogue would be required in order to agree on such a procedure and particularly to implement it.

In a recent article, "Where is the Church Going?," Harvey Cox has commented on the future of preaching:

A certain amount of *verbal reticence* will characterize the future style of Christians. The church has too often been seen by those outside as a talking and preaching organization—the place where one hears a long, boring disquisition, is hectored about one's moral failings or asked for money. It is frequently seen as a group of people fully equipped with quick and easy answers to questions no one is asking.[12]

Whether we speak of verbal reticence or a moratorium on preaching, the direction is clear—and that direction is away from the misuse we are now making of the sermon with our verbal libertinism. It is my feeling that in the future we will need to move away from the rigid preaching situation and toward new structures with the following features:

1. Worship in small mission-oriented task-force units, occasionally supplemented by mass meetings for special purposes

12 *United Church Herald,* January, 1967.

in larger, more impersonal groupings or congregations. This would allow worship to be more immediate, more personal, and more closely related to the actual life of that small group of persons. This worship would be more informal and more indicative of the life of the group, celebrating its joys, reflecting its tragedies, and seeking real help for real problems.

2. The increasing use of a variety of worship forms, including dance, drama, and silence in addition to some of the forms more familiar to us now.

3. Emphasis on the mutual responsibility of every Christian to share his faith, and witness to it in the midst of his fellow Christians, rather than focusing this responsibility on one man.

4. Emphasis on study of the Christian faith and its implications in small groups, rather than depending upon the sermon to educate the congregation on major issues. This would necessarily include the study of current social and political issues as well as matters of faith.

5. The occasional experience of a formal liturgical worship service, cathedral-style, with excellent music and outstanding preaching; rather than the watered-down attempt at this style week after week in churches with a lack of musical talent and a minister who preaches poorly. By adopting this style, the churches in a particular city or area could spend their time, energy, and money in more fruitful ways. We could cease the wasteful building of vast, expensive sanctuaries which are used for an hour or two each week, and divert our funds and energies to the service of our neighbors. One large meeting hall could serve a large area for these occasional festival gatherings.

What I am really proposing, then, is a simpler, more informal pattern of worship in smaller units, with a combination of silent waiting, verbal witnessing, and other modes of expression. A keynote must be the sharing of gifts and witnessing to the mighty acts of God by *all the people*. The Quaker style of silent worship together with witnessing by members of the group probably comes closer to this than any other current practice. I do not suggest that the entire Quaker approach be adopted for all churches, nor any other single style. There are many varieties of Quaker practice, and there is a discernible trend among them to combine preaching and silent worship in the same service. But it may be time for us to heed the witness these people have been quietly bearing. This witness is powerful at three points: (1) the spiritual value of silence, (2) the importance of mutual witnessing by all the members of the group, who share on a basis of equality, and (3) courageous action in the form of sacrificial service to the world. Quakers clearly do not have all the answers, but some modification of our approach to worship and proclamation in the light of their three-pronged witness may be a powerful step toward relevance.

If we took this worship style seriously, bringing to it the expertise and experience we have in other areas of church life, it could be a fruitful combination. It would mean that we could invest far less of our resources in costly buildings and unnecessary trappings. We would have less need of paid soloists and choirs. Our professional leadership in the churches could devote more time to genuine pastoral care, training of the laity, and teaching, rather than costly sermon preparation which is not yielding fruit in proportion to the time required.

My feelings about this style of worship are based on three factors. The first is my disillusionment with the barren patterns we are now pursuing. They have clearly lost their vitality, and we are only being dishonest with each other when we pretend that we find spiritual refreshment in these patterns, when, in truth, we do not. The second is the spiritually refreshing experiences I have had when worshiping with Quakers and others where silent worship was observed, including retreat experiences at places like Kirkridge and Pendle Hill. I find that many Protestant ministers are afraid to experiment with silent worship because they have never had an experience of it themselves, and do not know what to expect. The third reason I feel inclined to a style of mutual witness and silence in small groups is that it fits everything I know of communication theory.

In much of the literature on the renewal of the church, we read of the need to deepen our worship life as well as of reaching out in mission to the world. However, no one seems willing to give up the tired Sunday morning service as it currently exists in order to find more creative worship forms. Yet this may be precisely the key to that renewal we say we want so badly.

What are the biblical and theological foundations for such a scheme? I am convinced that there *are* solid biblical and theological foundations for a program of church life centered in mutual witness by all the people, rather than the paid weekly testimony of a professional speaker. That foundation is found expressed with great clarity in the current theological literature on the ministry of the laity.

The scriptural foundation for the ministry of the laity is found in passages like the fourth chapter of Ephesians. In this passage, it is clear that the early Christians all had gifts to share. Some were to be prophets, some evangelists, some pastors and teachers. These gifts were not all concentrated in one paid clergyman in the early church. In his careful, scholarly treatment of this theme, *Agents of Reconciliation*, Dr. Arnold B. Come has provided an excellent understanding of the church's need to return to a ministry of the whole people.[13]

Dr. Come presents another fascinating image of a tomorrow-structure. As he interprets the New Testament, and particularly Paul's message, the real heart of the Christian witness in the world comes through the day-to-day actions of Christians rather than our verbal statements about that faith. His discussion of this matter is worth careful study. He concludes:

> The startling and momentous implication follows, therefore, that Paul conceived of God's new covenant of reconciliation of the whole world as being ministered (mediated) not through the preaching of the Word and the administration of the sacraments within the church, but through the active wordless witness of the whole Christian community in its dynamic living relationships with all the world.[14]

Albert van den Heuvel is another who believes that the future of preaching lies in the direction of shared witness of all the people. He writes: "It seems to me that we have to go one step farther and say that *the renewal of the preaching ministry is the rediscovery of its communal character.*"[15] He goes on to say that the minister cannot preach alone. He not only needs the contribution of his people with their experience and questions to shape the message, but some of his laymen

---

13 *Op. cit.*
14 *Ibid.*, pp. 154–155.
15 *Op. cit.*, p. 71.

may be more gifted in *delivery* than he! "What a blessing for the tired chief executive of the congregation if his contribution to the preaching preparation is mostly theological!"[16]

So there is scriptural and theological precedent for a movement toward the mutual witness of every Christian. However, what if a solid scriptural footing for such a view did not exist? I firmly believe that God continues to reveal his truth and light to us in this present day, and that some of that new truth may well contradict the earlier revelations recorded in the Scriptures, even as some of those revelations contradict each other. We must proceed on faith to test new insights and new methods, or some of our most promising ventures may never get off the ground.

I confess that my personal experience and inclinations have strongly colored my view of the future of preaching. I happen to believe passionately in the ministry of the laity, and I find the quiet, unpretentious witness of the average man in a silent service often speaks to my spirit. There may be other possible styles that will emerge in the church of tomorrow that have equally as much power and potentiality. I offer this as one which makes sense to me in terms of my particular understanding and experience.

We are faced today with a situation in which the Protestant pulpit is psychologically empty! Its message is not being heard. It represents a great waste of time and energy as presently pursued. I yearn to see that vast reservoir of leadership energy freed for more significant ministries. And I yearn for more vital worship than we are currently offering our people. Whatever the communication style of the future turns

[16] *Ibid.*, p. 72.

out to be, perhaps the most crucial note is the importance of recapturing the gift of witness and proclamation from the clergy to be shared with the whole church again.

Those Christians gifted and called by God to preach, whether they be lay or clergy, let them be heard! And let us urge them to be the best possible preachers they can be, with thorough preparation and study. But let us not demand this gift of every minister whether he has it or not. Let us not deceive ourselves into idolizing preaching, and thereby smothering the other gifts of ministry.